CW00684691

The Thinking Rider

The Thinking Rider

Unlock your peak perfomance

by Dr Robert J Schinke

Copyright © 2006 by Cadmos Verlag, Brunsbek, Germany

Typesetting and design: Ravenstein and Partner, Verden, Germany

Printing: Westermann, Zwickau

Cover photograph: Atkins

Photos:

Atkins: pages 12-13, 19, 26-29, 32, 37-46, 51-57, 60-64, 69,
73, 74 (top), 75-93, 100, 107-118, 126-131, 136-156

Busch: page 20

Horse & Hound: pages 16, 21-22, 50, 59, 71, 74 (bottom),
95, 102, 122, 124, 134

Lenkeit: page 10

Schinke: pages 30, 34, 66, 106, 120

Cartoons: Paul Daviz

Edited by Jaki Bell

All rights reserved

Copying or storing in electronic or any other form is only
possible with the written permission of the publisher.

Printed in Germany

ISBN 3-86127-917-7

Table of content

Dedication

It is with the utmost humility that I dedicate this book to my wife, Erin. Without her, I would never have pursued my dreams as an academic, as a practitioner, and as a person. With Erin, an entire and expansive world has opened up to me. Thank you, my love.

Always and forever. **Rob**

Prologue

It has been nearly a decade since I co-authored Focused Riding, a mental training book for equestrians of all levels. Since then, I have completed a doctorate in the field of education, undergone extensive post-doctoral training in motivational psychology, and completed my national chartering as a mental training consultant. These academic certifications have opened the door to better understanding, and provided me with access to many national team and professional sport affiliates in Canada and worldwide. As with all people engaged in ongoing professional exploration, my views have both refined and altered with time. Initially, I believed that the most important sport psychology skills for the inspired athlete and coach were the mental training skills of relaxation, activation, focusing, imagery, goal-setting, self-talk, and planning. I still believe that generic mental training skills help riders, coaches, and their support-staff to maintain positive perspectives and consistent performances on the day to day, and in a wide variety of pressure filled situations. Now, however, I propose that anyone wishing to integrate sport psychology techniques look for answers using a wider repertoire of skills than those I referred to during my earlier book, Focused Riding.

This book

This book about the mental aspects of equestrian performance is intended to answer many of the questions that my previous book did not fully address. Several of those questions will be answered, with entire chapters devoted to the topics of
• sport confidence
• sport optimism
• optimal emotional management
• appropriate practising techniques, and
• the healthy performance perspective.

In the confidence chapter, a thorough explanation of how equestrian confidence works, and why only some people have confidence and hope as equestrians will be addressed.

Within the chapter devoted to optimistic equestrian thought, you will learn how explanations of past rides influence your long-term riding hopes and dreams. Equally important, suggestions will be provided regarding how you can develop a more positive viewpoint and a better long-term performance.

The chapter on emotions and self management will uncover some thinking, feeling, and physical indicators of strong and weak self-management.

The chapter on appropriate practicing techniques will reveal how riders and coaches can structure an optimal training environment to foster complete learning and a stellar bottom-line performance. Specific recommendations will be provided regarding how you can tailor schooling sessions to expedite learning and performance.

Also, an entire chapter is devoted to the healthy equestrian perspective. Perspective is an important aspect of equestrian performance. With it, riders, coaches and family members are tolerant, enthusiastic, and hopeful as they approach their day-to-day equestrian pursuits. I believe it necessary that all equestrians continuously refine and broaden their perspective. Only through a positive perspective can equestrian excellence be pursued over time. So, suggestions will be made regarding how you can maintain and develop the strongest of positive riding perspectives each day.

Clearly, there are many new and essential aspects to this equestrian sport psychology book. The additions discussed above will not take away from the importance of the mental training skills and applications that remain an integral part of this book. The favourite mental training topics of relaxation, arousal, imagery, goal-setting, self-talk and performance planning and implementation remain, and they too, are explored in-depth. The mental training applications that sustain as discrete chapters are more detailed than in my previous book, and provide you with a clearer explanation and set of suggestions regarding how best to integrate each skill. There will also be a thorough concluding chapter where I will tie up loose ends, and suggest how you can put your complete equestrian mental training package to work immediately. Enjoy this read, and enjoy your rides like never before!

My perspective

It is my wish to share with you a broadened perspective of the mental side of equestrian sport performance. I have worked with many of today's most successful professional and amateur elite athletes in many sports including equestrian. The skills out-lined in the chapters to come will guide you to improved equestrian performance. If you read this book and integrate its suggestions, your mental game will improve dramatically, I promise! The end result will be improved equestrian performance beyond what you ever anticipated. As a word of caution, though, remember that sport psychology skills are "waxed" skills. They require practice before they develop to a shine and lustre in the light of day. In essence, they have to see the light of day for some time before you can expect them to work at full intensity. Many aspiring riders and coaches are interested in the motivational side of equestrian performance. They attempt specific skills, use them with success once or twice, learn some interesting insights, and then forget what they have learned once performance returns to form. Top notch equestrian performance needs to be maintained through diligence and ongoing insights. When something works, take note and repeat it time and again. There is every reason to stick with what works and refine it into something better. In sport, the pursuit of excellence is ongoing. Enjoy the read and enjoy your ongoing journey toward development and satisfaction in the world of horses. You have chosen a great sport, and this book will re-emphasize that point time and again.

Robert Schinke, March 2006

Introduction

The last fifty years have been witness to increased growth in the area of sport psychology. As people take on increased interest in the mental aspects of performance, sport and business sectors worldwide have responded with motivational services. It is no longer difficult to find motivational consultants including corporate coaches and mental coaches. In university psychology and human kinetic departments, courses on motivation are usually packed with students looking for personal answers to sport and life performance. Most national and professional sport teams in North America engage the services of a mental training consultant to increase the probability that their athletes, coaches, and management perform at optimal levels. Why is there such an interest in the psychology of sport performance you might wonder? Simply put, it is always a challenge to perform optimally, even when performers have the technical training to do so. There are always surprise upsets in Olympic Games and professional sport venues. To think that the rise and fall of athlete performance on a given day can be explained by random luck or fate is a mistake. Differences in performance on a given day are often explained by thinking and mood, and how these facets translate into performance behaviours.

I have worked as a mental coach in elite sport for over a decade. Throughout, I have assisted successful international athletes and teams worldwide. Some of the more exciting events where the athletes and coaches I assist have gained medals have included Pan-American Games, World Championships and Olympics, among other highly regarded international tournaments. With professional sport, I have assisted athletes, coaches, and management for nearly five years. Many of the professional athletes I have worked with have become world champions, or at the very least, world top ten contenders in the sports of equestrianism, boxing, figure skating, golf, shooting, track and field, and ice-hockey, among others.

Every group I am part of tends to follow a similar lifecycle. All approach the mental aspects of sport performance with some scepticism. At the beginning of my first prestigious contract, I recall being told that I seemed like a nice guy, and that I would be allowed to join in on a pre-determined national team training camp because there were sport science allotted government funds that needed to be spent on sport psychology before the end of the fiscal year. With caution, the person in charge of the initiative, who has subsequently become a close friend, told me that sport psychology held little or no merit. I was hired for personal, not professional, reasons. More than a decade later I have learned to expect this somewhat pessimistic initial response as the typical reception encountered in my capaci-

When a rider and horse are performing at their peak, their mental approach and attitude can be the factors that give them the edge.

◎ Some riders approach competition with enhanced images of other competitors' performance that undermine their own prospects.

ty as mental training consultant. Few are the initial receptions that are trusting and optimistic.

With time, almost all of the people I have encountered through contracts consider the mental aspects of sport performance more seriously. There is no better a confirmation of mental training than when an athlete - coach combination succeed when they are not expected to. At that moment the mental training lights go on, the athletes along with their support systems begin subscribing in full measure. They become active participants in all exercises that shore up their pre-existing mental talents, and so, deeper learning and rewards follow synergistically. Some athletes are strong in goal-setting, but lack confidence. Others are strong in planning

and preparation aspects only to be sub-optimal in their ability to work seamlessly with their support. Still others are strong in their ability to image, but the pictures that they rehearse are undermining, and sometimes, debilitating. Many have the talent to perform beyond their own expectations, but fail to persist due to negative expectations or incorrect assignments of accountability. The list goes on.

Coaches face many of the same challenges that their athletes do. Perhaps this is why my consulting time is equally allocated to athletic, coaching, and managerial populations. Typically, the point of entry is one member of this interesting triad, be it a parent, a coach, or an athlete. Before long, however, all are active and synergistic members of an optimistic

◎ Whilst coach or athlete may be the first to recognise the need for motivational coaching, it is essential that all members of the support team, including parents and owners if applicable, recognize and support the conclusions.

and mentally strong performance team. It seems that the team approach to performance works best. Working with under-confident athletes, restoring their confidence, and then sending them back to a support system that cannot fully recognize and support positive change is both inefficient and ineffective.

Working with under-confident athletes, restoring their confidence, and then sending them back to a support system that cannot fully recognize and support positive change is both inefficient and ineffective.

Working with under-confident athletes, restoring their confidence, and then sending them back to a support system that cannot fully recognise and support positive change is both inefficient and ineffective.

Similarly, working on optimistic educational tactics with a coach only to have positive thinking undermined by parents or administrative staff is also less than effective. Success is a big picture project where everyone plays an important role. There will be some useful content for you in this book whether you are a rider, a coach, a family member, or even, a friend. You will be able to consider every chapter's content regardless of your specific vantage point and interest.

You might wonder when equestrianism will fully enter into our discussion. After all, this book is meant to be devoted to riders, coaches, and their supporting cast. I forgot to mention that though my consulting background stems from a wide number of amateur and professional sports my lifelong personal background is in the world of equestrianism. My father is an equestrian coach, my parents have run an international equestrian facility for nearly thirty years, and I am first and foremost an equestrian competitor and coach. Though I have coached less since becoming a university professor at Laurentian University, in Sudbury, Canada, I do ride daily, as does my wife. We are avid equestrians, avid competitors, and most important, avid horse lovers.

My earliest riding experiences began at the age of nine. As is typical of many an aspiring elite equestrian, I competed at the provincial / state level, and with some success, graduated to junior national and international competitions. As an adolescent, I was the Captain of the Ontario Young Riders Team, where I competed as team captain at the North and South American Championships four times in the discipline of three-day eventing. With an ongoing interest in equestrian, some diligent coaching, and a few talented horses, I competed at the senior level, as well. Some of my senior experiences included being a member of the 1987 Pan-American Games, being short-listed again for the Canadian Equestrian Team in 1991, and throughout, being a regular competitor at Federation Internationale Equestre (FEI) competitions. Most recently, I have returned to the sport of equestrianism, and due to professional and personal time demands, I now focus on FEI level dressage competition. Dressage has provided me with the perfect opportunity to practise what I preach, and call on sport psychology techniques first hand.

Throughout my assorted experiences as an equestrian athlete, I must confess that like many other equestrians, I struggled with the mental aspects of performance at crucial moments. I was often a great competitor one day, only to be sub-par the next day. It seemed that one day's successes could not predict the next day's ride. Some of the many challenges I have either experienced first hand, or witnessed among my own riding students and the riding students of fellow coaches are included in the examples that follow.

- Several riders, coaches, or rider-coach combinations have questioned their own abilities in crucial moments during schooling, or as they approached the competition ring.
- Other riders and coaches have experienced difficulties focusing their thoughts during their training and performances.
- I coached one international level athlete who was always thinking about riding when he was driving his car, and thinking about his studies while riding his horse.
- Other horse people never achieved their goals, in part because their goals were unclear, poorly monitored, or marred with both thinking errors at the same time.
- Among elite equestrians, some have struggled with anger management impulse concerns, and as a result, they have accidentally spur marked their horses and undermined their long-term horse - rider relationship. Many such riders struggled in crucial competitions when their horses anticipated harmful consequences for less than serious mistakes.
- Still other horse-rider combinations have been plagued by either overly relaxed or overly nervous responses to performance pressures. The result was an unresponsive horse, more intrigued by the rider's unusual signals, than the signals being asked by the rider.

Each of these examples might pinpoint a skill set that you, or one of the riders you are currently working with, or supporting, have struggled with. This book will provide answers to a wide number of mental training skills that are crucial to optimal equestrian performance. Every rider, coach, and support-staff member is different in terms of strengths and weaknesses. Throughout this book, you will gain an improved understanding of where you are strong, and where you are in need of refinement.

Each of us has room for change and refinement somewhere. Even the strongest of mentally tough athletes and coaches have areas that they can improve. As you are reading through this book, remember that the key to ongoing optimal performance is to build upon strengths and work on weaknesses. There is nothing wrong with being weaker in one area of your mental game, than in another. Weaknesses are opportunities to learn something new, and opportunities to become even better than you currently are. Imagine the opportunity to progress while exploring uncharted waters. Instead of backing away from areas where you are less certain, tackle head on the chapters you are less familiar with, or less proficient at. Far too

many athletes and coaches work mostly on their strengths. This book is written with skills that together provide a complete package. It is meant to solidify strengths, and shore up weaknesses.

General Tips

- Mental skills will enhance your equestrian pursuits through an improved positive and focused approach.
- Riders and coaches need to work on mental strengths and weaknesses equally.
- Mental skills work best when all members of the performance team including family members and friends work on them together.
- Mental skills require practise. If a specific skill does not work optimally at first, be persistent. It will work with practise.
- Once you have discovered a technique that works, don't forget that it works and discard it. Continue to use the mental training methods that helped you achieve optimal equestrian performance.

◎ "I coached one international level athlete who was always thinking about riding when he was driving his car"...

1. Developing equestrian confidence

In riding, confidence is a must. Beginner riders often struggle with confidence when mounting the unfamiliar assigned school horse. When riders attempt their first jumps, their first dressage tests, or experience their first rides outside the confines of an indoor arena, or outdoor in open fields, confidence is challenged once more. The first novice competition, the first international competition, and even the first Olympic Games can evoke self questioning for the rider or coach. Unfamiliar experiences, more challenging experiences than previously encountered, and challenges where setbacks were previously experienced tend to separate the optimally confident equestrian from the equestrian who struggles with self-doubt or doubt over horse ability. Challenges to confidence can be found at every level of equestrian expertise and every level of competition. Let's face it, in the world of horses there are many unknowns.

Have you ever watched Spruce Meadows Masters on television? Every autumn, my wife and I sit down in front of our television on the scheduled Sunday afternoon to watch the final international class. The stands are filled with people bused in by the thousands. The jumps are beautifully decorated, and the degree of jumping course difficulty is at its toughest. Spruce Meadows Masters is a wonderful testing ground of equestrian confidence. As the class unfolds, the performances of the international show jumpers seem to happen in ebbs and flows. If one rider - horse combination jumps a beautiful round, it often happens that several successful riders follow immediately after. Similarly, if a horse-rider combination experiences difficulties, or even a dramatic fall, the following riders enter the ring tentatively. They seem to hold their horses together tightly, hoping they can perform with more success than the rider who went before them. Facial expressions echo the emotional and thinking concerns felt first by the riders, and afterward, by their horses. And so, the afternoon progresses with a variety of performances, stemming from riders with different amounts of confidence.

In the sport of three-day eventing, the same pattern of ebbs and flows in rider confidence hold true, especially during the cross country phase. Refusals, run-outs, and falls are relatively common during the cross country phase. Obstacles are typically solid, and when met on an incorrect distance, sometimes result in a setback for the horse-rider combination,

Refusals, run-outs and falls during the cross country phase of a three-day event can cause ebbs and flows in rider confidence.

and perhaps for the horse-rider combinations that follow. The contrasting confidence of three-day event riders is seen during course walks, during warm-ups, when watching others compete, and as riders progress around their cross country courses. I have seen many a three-day rider walk a cross country obstacle countless times with a look of confusion and concern. Similarly, I personally walked many a cross country course in my time with varying anticipation of what was to come. I was more confident approaching some fences and some courses, as opposed to others. Sometimes I could see success, and sometimes I just could not. Other riders of all levels have also spent countless hours on a given fence trying to figure out how to jump it successfully. Some riders arrived at a solution, and in a few instances, I witnessed riders without solutions, even as they departed the starting box. Equestrian confidence is fluid, and every three-day event horse-rider combination, much like their show jumping cousins, has their confidence tested from time to time. Challenges to confidence are unavoidable in the sport of equestrianism.

Equestrian coaches also have their confidence tested from time to time. Coaches are faced with adversities of equal challenge to the horses and riders they work with. All coaches can recall instances where they anticipated both strong and less than optimal performances in their clients. The coach's confidence, much like the rider's confidence, can waiver depending on the degree of lesson or course difficulty, an unfolding of momentary circumstances, and perhaps, even as a result of personal circumstances. What I am trying to say is that coaches are people, too, and their beliefs sometimes vary. The coach's beliefs, in turn, are easily interpreted by the vulnerable rider, and afterward, felt by the attentive horse. The equestrian's momentary fluctuation in confidence can stem from many sources including other riders and personal coaches.

On a more general level, there are more and less confident coaches. Confident coaches oftentimes produce confident riders, who in turn produce confident horses. Less confident coaches tend to produce long-term self-questioning and uncertainty in the riders that they produce, especially when the riders progress to a reasonably challenging level. In a recent study I conducted, it became clear that world renowned athletes, including international equestrians, tend to draw a significant amount of confidence from their coaches, especially as the athletes progress from one level of performance to the next. When coaches question their own abilities, or the abilities of their horses and riders, limiting equestrian performance often results. There are many coaches with equal technical knowledge, and yet, varying degrees of success when it comes to producing horse-rider combinations. The ability to push oneself and others to the next level of performance is a skill that sometimes separates good and technically sound developmental coaches from great elite level coaches.

There is no denying the importance of confidence to horse-rider combinations, and to their coaches when considering short-term and long-term equestrian performance. This chapter has several purposes. First, it has been developed to clarify for you why some equestrians and their coaches are more confident than others. Some people falsely assume that people are born with a preset level of confidence, either strong or weak. This is not the case. Second, many assume that confidence in the moment just happens as a result of determination. Again, many of us underestimate the systematic nature of performer confidence. We will explore how equestrian confidence ought to be developed. I have witnessed many examples where horse and rider confidence was intended, but aspired to using incorrect and faulty techniques. There is a highly effective confidence framework that has been confirmed time and

◎ The ability to push oneself and others to the next level of performance is a skill that separates good coaches from great coaches.

again in sport, and in life. The confidence framework you are about to read illustrates how riders and coaches can develop and teach confidence to each other and their horses effectively, and cumulatively. Third, suggestions will be provided regarding how to restore confidence in the confidence depleted equestrian performer. There are many horse and rider combinations with all of the technical skills to achieve their objectives,

other than the often intangible attribute of confidence. This chapter will provide suggestions regarding how to develop your equestrian confidence, and the equestrian confidence of those you work with. I recommend that you read this chapter slowly and carefully. It will come in handy personally in your schooling and performance with horses, or when helping a student or friend aspire to ongoing riding improvements.

This team are obviously enjoying their performance but some competitors can find the pressure of the show ground very different from that of the practice arena at home.

◎ Recollection of past successes, at whatever level, helps to build winning future performances.

How confidence works

Over the last thirty years, one of the leading confidence researchers has been Albert Bandura, an eminent psychology professor and researcher from Stanford University. Indirectly, Bandura has provided sport enthusiasts, including equestrians, with a framework through which to understand how sport confidence works. There are two easily applicable basic ground rules that help explain equestrian confidence.

First, each coach or rider has a specific belief in the likelihood of meeting performance demands in each context. When riders arrive in the arena, and are faced with a specific jumping or dressage exercise on a specific day, they will have a specific and momentary amount of confidence regarding the likelihood of completing the exercise successfully. Second, every equestrian's confidence can vary as the degree of exercise difficulty is altered; meaning that riding confidence alters as the exercise is made easier or more difficult, or as the context becomes more controlled or more dis-

tracting. Some riders, for instance, are relatively confident when jumping a course of three foot obstacles in a quiet indoor arena. When the same riders are asked to jump the exact same course outdoors in a show setting, where there are more distractions, excitement, and intangibles, their confidence wavers.

What the second ground rule indicates, then, is that equestrians can vary in their confidence when asked to fulfill the very same task in easier and more complex performance settings. Confidence for the equestrian is not set in stone - it can change from one context to the next and from one moment to the next depending on performer interpretation.

Four ways to gain equestrian confidence

Think back to a riding scenario wherein you were completely confident, and as a result, approached your student or your horse with the utmost sense

Watching successful riders complete challenges with skill will
provide you with a positive mental picture on which to base your ride.

of belief and purpose. You just knew that things were going to unfold successfully, and all the people around you were able to notice your quiet though solid sense of purpose and knowing. I can recall horse shows, and even seasons of horse shows when I just knew that I was going to give my best, and perform at the highest level. If you haven't experienced that complete sense of belief with horses, you undoubtedly have when writing a test or exam, when debating with a friend or colleague, and even when applying for that special job. If you can recall a moment of complete confidence, did that solid sense of self-confidence stay with you indefinitely? It seems that confidence is not a constant for most riders and coaches, regardless of whether it is within sport, or otherwise. The most common question that riders and their coaches always ask me is could they teach themselves, their horses, or their students to be more confident? I always respond with a smile, a yes, and a strong belief that I can answer their question.

We all have experienced the ebbs and flows of confidence, we all have used at least a few of the contributing sources to confidence, few of us have developed our confidence using the widest number of contributing sources, and even less have used these sources effectively. Take a second and reflect over that special moment when you rode or coached with that complete sense of certainty. Do you think that positive equestrian performance just happened? What sorts of things needed to be in place before you performed with a high level of confidence? If you are unable to retrace the thoughts and actions that contributed to a high level of self-confidence in riding, think about a riding situation where you performed with a complete lack of self-confidence. What sorts of factors contributed to your lack of belief? Take 10 minutes and consider the things that added to or diminished your sense of belief.

I will bet money that you identified at least one of the following four sources of information as contributing factors when recalling your performance:

- a recollection of personal past experiences;
- reflections of other riders' good or bad performances;
- your support-system's advice, suggestions, and beliefs; or
- your ability to control your thoughts and emotions before and during the performance.

For the ideal positive thinking rider, all four of these confidence sources can be integrated effectively into a confidence building plan. If you are a rider who struggles with confidence, I am prepared to wager that you use the very same techniques as the more confident rider, but in your case, they are used to undermine your positive thinking. Following is an explanation of how to use each confidence source the way it is meant to be used, effectively.

Past experiences

Every rider, coach, and horse develops beliefs about the future likelihood of success based on past memories. After all, what could be more confirming of future performance expectations than previous similar experiences? The confident equestrian will tend to recall many positive and confirming experiences from the past. The less confident rider will tend to recall personally undermining past performances. I assisted an aspiring equestrian the year before the 2003 Pan-American Games. The rider was initially uncertain regarding her prospect of performing at the highest level, internationally. She provided a wide variety of reasons and past experiences that would have undermined my confidence as well. The first forward moving discussion that we had was an exploration of previous recent top performances, where the rider performed to her potential. As the discussion proceeded, we worked together and I documented as many details as she provided regarding her winning rides from pre-performance training, through her competition warm-ups, through ring tactics, through her thoughts and emotions leading up to each performance and while she was performing. As the discussion progressed, I noticed a transition in the rider's emotions, her facial expression, and even her posture. She became positive, hopeful, receptive, taller, and yes, more confident. Because the rider was from overseas, we met intermittently, and our focus was solely on how to think positively. The result was an unexpected individual medal at the Pan-American Games, and a best ever performance during a crucial moment. Though past successful experiences are not the only answer to improved confidence, more time has to be devoted to thinking about good rides, and less time ought to be devoted to thinking about and replaying bad rides.

There are also instances where no suitable past experiences can be recalled. Take for instance the rider who has never jumped before today's request. All riders are faced with unfamiliar circumstances from time to time. First experiences galloping, first dressage shows, first jumping shows, first regional or national finals, or a successful experience to compare with the aforementioned. During circumstances when you experience uncharted waters, you need to look to the other three sources of confidence enhancing information to guide you to first-hand success. After all, if you haven't experienced the challenge yet, or haven't experienced success at it yet, there are others you can watch, others who can guide you, and at very least, there are optimal ways to manage your thoughts and emotions to increase your chance of success. All is not lost when you undertake challenges that you have yet to succeed at. Resourceful people, including resourceful riders need to look beyond what they don't have,

to the confidence enhancing information sources that are available to them. Building confidence is a creative endeavor that is fun, rewarding, enlightening, and highly possible.

Observing riders

There is no doubt that watching other riders of an equal performance level, either succeeding or struggling, can influence your sense of belief.

So how can you watch others in a way that builds upon your confidence? I can recall an international Young Riders competition that I attended with my father, who was also my coach. It was a very hot and sunny cross country day, and we wanted to watch the more experienced senior competitors complete a series of water jumps that I would have to ride later on that day. My father and I witnessed a succession of five international riders approach the series of jumps with too much speed. The result was five consecutive horse and rider combinations falling in the water. My father looked at my face, and knew that the decision to watch these weak performances shortly before I had to compete was a bad one. After all, how was I to successfully complete the series of obstacles, if more experienced and competent riders with more experienced horses could not? Just as my father was deliberating how best to foster my confidence given what I had just observed, a less experienced horse and rider combination recently graduated from the Young Riders division approached the series of fences, and jumped them with no effort. The picture was perfect! I was whisked away to the stables where my horse was tacked and waiting. With that final successful picture in my mind, I approached the fence the same way, experienced the same success, and went on to complete that competition with two horses among the top four in that prestigious national competition.

Most of us would agree, then, with the saying that a picture means a thousand words. I want to refine that statement a little more to ensure that you have a clear guide of exactly what kind of picture will give you or your students the biggest bang for the dollar. If you lack previous successful experience in the exercise or skill level that you are currently hoping to attempt, there are specific guidelines that you can consider when using observation as a performance enhancement tool. First of all, you need to watch successful riders completing the same task or a similar task to the one you are attempting. Obviously, watching a negative image might contribute to learning, but it will not contribute to increased confidence. Second, the rider that is being observed needs to either be at your level, or only slightly above your level. To observe a world renowned competitor complete a task comparable to your own can provide a beautiful model of what to do, but that form of observation will not increase your sense of momentary self-belief as you face the very same challenge. Third, the horse-rider combination being observed should be of similar physique and style. This latter point will contribute a little more realism to the model you are observing and hoping to copy. Ultimately, it is best if you can eventually picture yourself as successful before attempting whatever challenge you have chosen to face. The best way to picture yourself succeeding is by observing someone of comparable physique, body strength and dexterity. If you lack access to appropriate models at your own stable, ask the owner of another stable with comparable riders whether you can video their riders during training. You can also gain a wonderful video library by recording the performances of similar riders during competition, if competing is your interest. Together, these suggestions will increase the likelihood that you can use observational learning to your best advantage.

Creditable persuasion

All coaches would agree that they sometimes use persuasion to push their riders to the next level. I am certain that you have first hand experience with someone pushing you successfully out of the comfort zone. Can you recall the first time your coach asked you to canter, gallop, jump, ride in an open field, or compete in a challenging class? How about the first time you were asked to jump an obstacle that you were a little intimidated by? Where was your coach at those moments? If your coach was there, and said: "You can do it, go!" I will bet that you were more likely to grit your teeth, try each

◎ "What if the person who was trying to convince you was someone you didn't trust?"

◎ Sometimes "You can do it" needs to be backed up with more specific advice.

new challenge, and as a result, extend the boundaries of your experiences so that they included a wider repertoire of skills, or the same skills at a more challenging level. All great coaches have the ability to help push their athletes out of the comfort zone from time to time.

What would have happened if the person who was trying to persuade you knew little or nothing about riding? What if the person trying to convince you was someone you didn't trust? It seems that persuasion works in riding, but that the persuaders need to have a few characteristics in order for their enticements to work. Obviously, in equestrianism,

the effective persuader needs to have a strong base of riding knowledge. Every now and again, riders are exposed to persuasive suggestions from a person who has yet to acquire the appropriate level of experience. Your probable response, which would be typical and fair, is to ignore and disregard the suggestion. After all, what does an inexperienced riding person know about the equestrian challenges that you are currently facing? Additionally, if you are to be persuaded, you obviously need to respect the persuader's credibility regardless of whether he or she has a sufficient base of equestrian knowledge. People can, after all, have a lot of experience, while not having the right experiences to help you! There is more to credibility than experience, then. There is also judgment. Experience without adequate judgment is an incomplete package when it comes to persuading sport performers. To be sold the idea that you can jump that fence, gallop that course, or ride that horse, when there is a less than optimal belief in self, you need to believe in the person persuading you, and put your faith in their hands.

A few years ago, I walked a relatively challenging national level show jumping course with a developing and talented show jumper who I coached. The rider had never competed in an open jumping class, and when we walked the course, he continuously monitored my expression and words, seeking to gauge my belief in him. As we examined the challenges to be faced that Sunday, I knew that my rider was ready. His horses were well schooled and he had all of the technical capabilities to manage the day's challenges. All that was missing was a sense of certainty on the rider's part. Knowing full well the need for creditable persuasion, I provided the aspiring Young Rider with specific tactical suggestions, some positive reinforcement, and topped off the advice with a smile that exuded confidence. As the warm-up progressed, I provided the rider with a few specific reminders, and I slowly assisted him as he built his confidence for this new and revealing moment. The rider entered the ring in a solid rolling canter, waited for the bell, and got down to business. The course revealed what I already knew and more. Not only did my rider complete the course, he made it to the jump-off with both of his horses, and claimed a healthy share of the prize money that day. With that initial successful experience in hand, the rider's confidence became increasingly self-directed as the season progressed.

What is the key to effective persuasion, you might wonder? As we discussed earlier, obviously, the person delivering the message must be viewed as cred-

itable. There is more to strong and motivating persuasion than that, however. Every riding coach delivers a wide array of information, both spoken and unspoken. In terms of what is spoken, clearly, the nervous and questioning rider cannot absorb great amounts of persuasion. After all, often at the moment when persuasion is sought, the rider is struggling with an elevated heart rate, and vivid images about a wide number of potential riding outcomes, both good and bad. The best sort of feedback when being persuaded in a crucial moment includes a balance between inspiration, specific technical suggestions, and simplicity. I have witnessed many a riding coach say to their concerned riders: "You can do it". More specific advice was needed. The short-term response of the rider provided with general motivated suggestions is always: "How?" Clearly, confidence building equestrian coaches needs to have a few specific suggestions, or pathways to success up their sleeves when supporting the progress of their riders. Persuasion without specific suggestions is not persuasive at all.

There are other coaches who in a moment of pressure provide such detailed input that their athletes become lost in the details. Have you ever experienced too much detail when you were under the pressure of performance? What were you able to retain? You probably recall little other than the nervously delivered information of your coach. Even when equestrian coaches are highly knowledgeable, much of what they say can be lost in translation with too much detail packed into a few seconds. The overly nervous rider and horse combination could probably absorb a few words effectively during a trying moment, and no more. As the saying seems to hold true when trying to effectively instill confidence within the crucial moment, "genius is in simplicity". If you are a riding coach, simplify your suggestions in pressure filled moments. If you are a rider, make certain that your coach targets a few words that you can integrate.

When there is less momentary pressure, and there is no consequence in taking a few extra minutes to absorb and integrate coaching detail, then take the extra time necessary to understand and integrate the information that will take you that next step in riding performance.

Confidence delivered by a coach, or another creditable person, can also come from unspoken information. Have you ever experienced a coach telling you that she believes in you, and when you looked into her eyes, you knew she was telling you the truth? There was a sense of calmness, wisdom and certainty that you interpreted from her posture, facial expression, and eye contact. On the other hand, have you ever experienced someone telling you that you were capable, and you intuitively knew that there was no belief behind the message? I remember debriefing a group of international level athletes after they fell short in an important competition. I interviewed several of the athletes for both applied and research use, and all shared the same interesting interpretation: they noticed at crucial moments that their well regarded elite coach's eyes and posture indicated a lack of belief despite her words. It seemed that she was trying to mask her lack of belief instead of entertaining more positive outcomes. When pushing yourself to the next level of performance, or when attempting a riding skill in a challenging circumstance, you are best supported by the coach who exudes confidence in both words and actions. Persuasive words need to be delivered methodically, and guess what; facial expressions, eye contact and posture need to be convincing, too!

Self control

To develop or improve your riding confidence, you can also work from the inside out, starting with your own body and mind responses. Sometimes, you might come across a challenge unlike anything you have ever faced before, there is no one to model, and the support of someone else is not available. Also, there will be instances as a rider when you will have positive past experiences to draw on, positive models, positive persuasion, and yet, you will still feel nervous. With both examples, your self-control will be as important as any other skill set that you can use to your advantage as an equestrian. Your ability to manage nerves, breathing, and thinking to a level that works best for you, cannot be underestimated.

You hold the ability to manage yourself successfully when faced with stressful and challenging moments based on past life experiences. I am certain that you, like me, have managed yourself both effectively and ineffectively when faced with life's challenges. If all cumulative experiences were to result in progressive learning, we would both be experts in self-management! Do you have a strong understanding of the self-control strategies that work best for you when you are nervous or challenged? With a fast approaching riding competition, or a momentary challenge posed in a schooling session, do you always manage your focus, concentration, and perspective optimally? If you do, you have obviously learned a great deal about how you respond in a wide number of performance settings. You undoubtedly know the sorts of thoughts, emotions, and behaviours that work best for you as a rider. I am certain that you also have a wide number of strategies that you use when moving toward excellent self-management. Large portions of self-knowledge most certainly increase your self-confidence.

◎ There are occasions, such as waiting in the start box before tackling a
cross-country course, when you will need to be able to manage your stress.

A Personal Anecdote

Some years ago when I was an aspiring international competitor, I took a series of show jumping lessons from an eminent equestrian, and eight-time Olympian, Ian Millar. Millar has won many grand prix show jumping competitions including the largest purse competitions, two Pan-American Games, two World Cup Finals, and the Alternate Olympics, in 1980. When I was schooling with Millar, I noticed that nothing fazed him. He was confident beyond belief. In between jumping rounds, he was able to joke with all of his disciples, me included. It was clear to me why he was so successful. He was able to focus when he was riding, relax when he was taking a break, and even laugh at himself when he was teased. He was an incredible example of positive thinking and self-control. The one question I wondered was whether he was able to maintain the same high level of composure and behaviours during a challenging competition.

A few months later, that question was answered. I met Ian again when we were both selected for the 1987 Canadian Pan-American Games Team for our respective disciplines. As I approached Ian at lunch on site, he was in the midst of yet another of his many jokes, this time at the expense of one of his younger teammates. He seemed as composed as when I met him at his farm earlier that year. The week progressed, his composure remained, and I knew that he was heading for another excellent result. Yet again, Ian won team and individual gold medals. Though I never asked Ian why he was so consistent, it was cleat that he was as relaxed under adversity as he was without adversity. He has become a glowing equestrian example of what exemplary self-management truly means to confidence and performance.

◎ Robert Schinke competing in the 1987 Pan-Am Games Advanced Section Trial.

Poor self-control is often linked with a loss of temper directed toward the horse, arguments with the coach, teammates, family, and friends, as well as personal frustrations. Have you ever experienced or witnessed out of control equestrians? There is nothing more infuriating to the rider than the recognition that self-control is lost. Beyond being personally dangerous, a lack of self-control will definitely undermine the rider's self-confidence. Ultimately, without self-control, the rider will become an inconsistent performer with a smaller number of positive past experiences to recall. Equally important, the rider who has yet to acquire strong and consistent self-management skills will suffer from an incomplete horse-rider relationship. The inconsistent rider will produce an inconsistent and untrusting horse. Complete rider development requires two types of consistency: technical consistency, and the sort of consistency we are considering now, emotional consistency. The strong technical rider will never be a consistent rider until his or her emotional and thinking approach is consistently positive and solution oriented.

You are probably wondering "how do I achieve optimal riding self-management?" As you have noticed, I have only spoken of self-control in general descriptive terms to this point in the book, and there is a good reason why. The remaining chapters are devoted to different aspects of self-control. The chapter devoted to optimism addresses self-control through constructive interpretations. Chapters are also devoted to imagery, concentration, relaxation, and activation. The chapters about simulation and competition planning also target unique aspects of self-control for the equestrian. The answer to your questions will not come all at once. Your understanding of optimal equestrian performance and self-management will come in smaller building blocks that together will build quite a foundation. I suggest that you work progressively through the rest of this book in order to ensure that all of your mental skills are at their best. However, if you need to focus on specific aspects immediately, develop a priority timeline starting with the most important chapters, and ending with the remaining equestrian mental training skills.

General Tips

- Use as many of the four sources of confidence developing information as you can when building your belief as an equestrian.
- Remember that confidence during easier riding challenges does not necessarily predict confidence in more challenging tasks.
- When you lack riding confidence, seek assistance from a confident and creditable coach/riding expert.
- You can also develop your riding confidence by using the very same strategies that have worked successfully for you in the pursuit of excellence elsewhere in life.
- Target at least two types of confidence enhancers each week. Recall past experiences, watch only positive and comparable riders, seek assistance from the coaches you trust most, and work on your self-management skills.
- If you are a coach of an under-confident rider, integrate as many of the four sources of confidence developing information with the aspiring rider as you can before and during training.

2. The optimistic equestrian

Have you ever heard such sayings as "always look on the bright side of life" and "honey attracts more flies than vinegar"? Both of these old adages hint at the importance of positive over negative thinking. As you would probably agree by this point, the way we think and the way we perform go hand in hand. Some people see all of the personal and interpersonal possibilities in life, and then they move forward and strive to achieve. Others get caught up in the barriers that stand between them and success. People's views of the world trickle into every aspect of their lives. Have you ever discussed the weather with friends? On a beautiful day, some point out the clouds in the sky, and others tend to point out the patches of clear blue sky. Both people could be speaking of the very same sky and the very same weather during the very same moment. Amazing isn't it? What a contrast in perception! How could both people be staring at the very same sky, and see two totally opposite worlds? Interestingly enough, two people can see the very same thing and look at it in their own unique way be it a challenge, a person or an animal. Furthermore, the way people interpret their life events or the events that are going on around them contribute to differences in their approach to performance, and so, to their success. In sport, perception is at very least just as important to performance as ability.

In riding, some equestrians approach their horse related activities through a lens that emphasizes blue sky. Others use a lens through which they focus on the clouds first and blue sky second. I spend a lot of my consulting time working with amateur and professional athletes, and their coaches in the area of sport perception. Some of the many riders I know provide all of the reasons why they are going to experience difficulties in an upcoming competition. Dressage riders readying for a competition might complain about the upcoming show's organization, its grounds, its staff, its judges, and even its organizers. Problem oriented show jumping riders sometimes focus on poor course design and overly soft or hard footing. Equestrians hoping to be selected to their national team, regardless of discipline, are sometimes consumed by all of the potential politics that stand in the way of selection and success. After listing a wide range of concerns, riders from all disciplines and all levels of experience who adopt a problem oriented perspective actually talk themselves into frustration, a decline in effort and so a decline in success. After all, why bother trying to perform your best when the chances of succeeding are slim to none? It is sometimes easiest to under-achieve, and then to assign accountability elsewhere.

Dressage riders with a positive focus will relish the opportunity of informed and competent judging during their dressage test.

 As a teenager the author believed cross country designers, amongst others, were there to thwart his competitive attempts. By the time he was walking this course in 1988 at the Fairhill Advanced Horse Trials this negative thinking was a thing of the past.

Others view their chances of equestrian success in a more positive way. Some dressage riders look forward to the opportunity of competent judging exposure and self-development. Some three-day event riders choose to focus on the adventure and excitement associated with their sport. With both of these positive thinking examples, more time is spent focusing on momentary and long-term dreams, and interestingly, the scope of optimistic dreams is without boundaries. Have you ever met riders who provide you with a whole list of reasons why they are going to succeed? Positive thinking riders will regard themselves and their horses as highly capable, and the circumstances around them as contributors instead of deterrents to ongoing success. Just being around positive and solution oriented equestrians is motivating! Positive perceptions in equestrianism are performance enhancing and contagious. After all, how can we help but to be excited and persistent when the possibilities for performance and success are endless?

Positive perceptions in equestrianism are performance enhancing and contagious.

I am devoting an entire chapter to the topic of positive thinking in equestrianism. My rationale for doing so is both academic and applied. Over the last decade, I have spent considerable time conducting research with positive and negative thinking athletes, including equestrians. What I have learned is worth sharing because it has helped many aspiring athletes exceed their goals as novices, amateur world champions, and professional world champions. This chapter on optimism and pessimism is meant to provide you with some insights regarding how people, including you, interpret equestrian performances, and the effects of those interpretations on riding development in the short- and long-term. Also of note, the optimism and pessimism dis-

A Personal Anecdote

I must confess that I began my riding career as a negative thinker. I was a cautious performer who worried about all of the potential barriers that stood in between me, my horse, and successful performance. As a teenager, I walked my cross country courses many times in order to convince myself that I was a capable rider. My father was always frustrated with my self-handicapping behaviours. It was clear to him that I had all of the required skills to be the best performer at most every domestic equestrian competition that I entered. Yet, I often under-rode dressage tests, incurred time faults cross country, and rode conservatively while show jumping. The habit of conservative and under-achieved performance was no accident. There were many dressage judges who I believed were saboteurs, there were several cross country course designers who I believed did not design appropriate courses, and there were several organizers and tack stewards who I believed did not like me. Just the thought of those potential competition barriers ended in a lowering of personal goals, effort, persistence, and self-fulfilling results for me. I had a negative view of competitive riding, and it trickled into my equestrian attitude, my results, and my ability to learn as a horseman and competitor. I was not the best student of equestrian sport during my early years.

 There is no obstacle that can't be resolved with a little creative thinking.

I now approach all sorts of performance in a very different way. Instead of being a problem oriented person, I have become solution oriented. There is no obstacle that can't be resolved with a little creative thinking. Misbehaving horses are no longer "problem horses" they are horses with a few weaknesses that require refinement. Schooling problems are regarded as a necessary part in the ongoing horse - rider partnership. Riding student problems are no longer indicative of poor athlete disposition. Athletes are now entitled to bad days and mis-understandings, as am I. Riders and coaches are approached and assisted in the very same way. Problems never overtake solutions anymore. Problems are temporary, and trimmed down to their correct size; they are not all-consuming. My approach to riding and life is now uplifting, hopeful, and inspiring. Solution oriented thinking is the exact philosophy that I bring to the table when helping riders ride to their best ability regardless of their level and aspiration. I have learned that for athletes, all of the correct technical and tactical skills couched in a pessimistic perspective will only end in under-achievement, disappointment, and sometimes, premature abandonment.

cussion that we are about to engage in can provide you with some wider suggestions regarding how to be a solution oriented thinker in riding, and in life. You have everything to gain from developing or refining your optimistic riding perceptions! Read on.

Research background

More than thirty years a go, a friend and colleague of mine started conducting research about how our interpretations of life events influence our willingness to excel in all aspects of life. Martin Seligman, a world renowned psychology professor from the University of Pennsylvania deduced that those of us with problem oriented perceptions learn to view our life events in a very different way from those of us who are solution oriented. Further, Seligman's research indicated time and again that our views of life's events seem to determine how much we persist when we are faced with challenges. Imagine that. The way we look at our experiences and circumstances has a strong influence on our willingness to persist, and so, our success in everything, including our riding endeavors! When considering the loss of potentially talented riding coaches, students and competitors at every level and in every equestrian discipline, I have learned that the loss of equestrian talent caused by negative thinking habits is quite profound. It is also preventable.

Over the last few years optimism research has found its way into equestrian sport psychology through mental training consultants, coaches and athletes. There are specific ways of thinking that motivate equestrians, and teach them how to view their sporting pursuits constructively. The skills I am speaking of are termed resilience skills, and you won't have any problem learning them quickly. I have taught solution oriented thinking skills to athletes and coaches as part of week-long training camps! The result is always the same; higher levels of performance than previously imaginable. The underlying message is clear: the more energy devoted to positive solutions, the better. The first national team that I taught resilience skills to moved forward and integrated their newly refined thinking as all but two athletes medalled at a World Championship in 2001! That year, I restricted my prac-

tice to less than 30 international amateur and professional athletes, and more than two thirds of the athletes achieved top three world rankings. Since then, I have assured athletes and coaches alike that positive thinking is pivotal when it comes to sport performance. Wonderful results and advances in performance stem from positive thinking, persistence, increased effort, and success in a synergistic way.

How optimism works

Despite the availability of optimism skills, I continue to come across a wide number of negative thinking equestrians at all levels, and so the discussion about optimism is revisited time and again. Typically, the conversations start with most riders or coaches believing that they are positive thinkers. A coach might say: "I give my riders lots of compliments. I believe rider X is a great rider, and I tell her so all of the time. How can what I am saying be interpreted as anything but positive? I am definitely a positive coach." Riders might provide similar responses. They might say: "I love my horse and I love my sport. I ride every day, and all of my friends are riders. I am a positive rider." Both examples of equestrian response seem reasonably positive, at least initially. Many of us consider ourselves as highly optimistic people. Yet, if you sit in and observe a riding lesson, or a horse show, you will be surprised to find that equestrians range on a continuum from being extremely problem oriented in their focus, to others who are moderately problem oriented, and still to others who are relatively solution oriented. This observation also holds true for coaches, riding families, and friends. Not all of us are entirely solution oriented, and as a result, not all of us progress with our equestrian development as rapidly as we should.

◎ At the end of your ride, take a few moments to evaluate the quality of the session in detail.

To understand where your perception resides in general terms, you can use a very simple framework with three main guidelines, or criteria: Is the performance regarded as permanent or impermanent? Is the performance explained by internal or external factors? Is the performance explained by domain specific or more general factors? All three of these criteria will be considered one at a time in relation to riding performance. While you are reading through each criterion, consider both a previous positive and negative riding experience.

Criteria One: Explaining circumstances in terms of their permanence

During and after finishing your ride each day, do you take a moment to evaluate the quality of the session? I will bet that on some level, intentional or unintentional, you do reflect on each ride in terms of its day to day permanence. After a good ride, you might think 'this is a great ride like usual' or 'this is an unusually good ride.' The very same interpretation tends to happen after a weaker riding experience. You response might be 'it is typical for this sort of ses-

response might be 'it is typical for this sort of session to go poorly' or 'how unusual to experience such a bad ride when practising this skill. We are both usually so strong at it.' Take a second and consider today's ride, if you've already ridden. Which one of the four general responses did you have? Did you have a good ride interpreted as usual or unusual, or a weaker ride interpreted as usual or unusual? Your evaluation of today's ride and, in fact every day's ride in terms of its permanence, can play a very interesting role on how you approach a similar riding performance next time.

In order to improve your optimism and your persistence, good performances need to be explained to permanent factors, or factors that can become permanent factors with some technical and psychological effort. Good rides don't just happen on the day. They need to be considered as the result of specific skills and specific decisions. I recall working with one inconsistent though talented athlete who believed that success was unpredictable as he prepared to qualify for the 1996 Olympics. When he performed well beyond expectation during earlier international tournaments and during the Olympic qualifiers that year, he said that he was 'on' during those days. Though I wasn't experienced enough to understand the implications of his post-performance self-evaluations, it was clear that his expectations of future success sounded questionable and temporary. At the Olympics, as I intuitively predicted earlier that year, the athlete returned to his self expected standards, and produced a performance that was a significant decline from his earlier successful performance. Why? He chose not to examine the specific technical and psychological behaviours that he integrated during his earlier optimal experiences. Instead, he incorrectly assumed that good and bad performances are typically unpredictable and fluid.

The key to permanent optimal performance is a complete understanding of what to do and how to do it. When a good friend of mine, Cindy Ishoy, recalled her successful performances from the 1988 Summer Olympic Games in Seoul, Korea, it was clear that she anticipated her success well in advance of her startling success in both the team and individual dressage competitions. Approaching the Olympic Games, Cindy and her mount Dynasty had accumulated strong results at the 1986 World Championships, at two World Cup Finals, and at the 1988 Olympic qualifiers. She believed that she and her mount were of the highest world class calibre, and that she had every reason to anticipate success. Approaching the 1988 season, she had a brilliant season-long competition plan designed for peak performance at the Olympic Games, and she had a well-established preset warm-up routine for each competition day. Everything was in place, and she believed that the end result was foreseeable and inevitable. As a result, Cindy rode Dynasty to second place individually and a bronze medal in the team competition, and to a top four finish in the individual competition a few days later. To this day Cindy and Dynasty's results are amongst the best achieved by North American dressage combinations at the Olympic Games.

Learning from the very best of equestrians such as Cindy, the rule of thumb in riding and in life is to explain your past successes and your future performances as foreseeable, with earlier performances used as confirming evidence that things will go well in later performances. With each success it is also necessary to follow your predictions of consistent excellence with detailed planning and diligence. The result, even during the toughest of riding challenges, will be reaffirming success and increased confidence and persistence. Success doesn't just happen, it is predicted, it is managed, and it is pursued.

Just as you have good rides and good performances, you probably also experience rides that are less than optimal. Ideally, when poor rides are experienced, they are meant to be interpreted in a constructive and impermanent way. There are always reasons why weaker riding performances happen. They can be the result of a bad day at work or school, a fight with a friend or family member, a poorly planned or managed schooling session, an overly worked and fatigued mount, personal fatigue, or poorly fitted tack, among a wide number of other factors. Many of the factors that end in weak rides are usually foreseeable and easily resolved, at least when we examine our rides after the fact. Just the same, if you listen to riders interpreting their sub-par rides, interpretations of the day's events can be placed on a continuum from permanently reoccurring to temporary and short-lived.

Riders in the process of interpreting their weaker rides negatively will typically assign their setbacks to their own typical behaviors, the typical behaviors of their mount, or both. Weak rides that are assigned to permanent factors will typically be supported by a wide range of previous rides that were also negative. The novice cross country rider who experiences a refusal for the second consecutive lesson on ditches might say: "You see. I told you I can't jump ditches." I have heard similar explanations from developing show jumping riders who've said: "My horse and I

don't like open water fences, and we don't like grass footing." Riders who interpret their weak rides or weak performances as permanent will tend to focus on, relive, and confirm previous negative rides. Earlier negative riding experiences are then regarded as all that was experienced in the past, even when that is not truly the case. Earlier negative rides become all that can be forecasted for the future, especially given the biased and debilitating evidence that is being used to confirm ongoing sub-par riding experiences.

Rides that are less than optimal can also be evaluated in a more constructive and impermanent way. You would be correct in your interpretations if you explained sub-par rides and poor competitive performances as temporary. Ultimately, when a setback is evaluated as a short-term learning experience, there is more reason to hope for better results, and so, to persist. Take a moment and think back to a ride that was sub-standard where you responded with the thought 'this is just a bad ride.' What were you saying to yourself? Whether you realized it or not, you were reminding yourself that the ride was unusually sub-par, and that there was little cause for concern. Using a positive interpretation of the day's events,

Viewing problems, both in the school or during competition, as temporarily sub-par enables a rider to move on, using the experience as part of future training strategies.

you were more likely to approach the following day's training, and your horse in the process, with a more confident attitude. The inevitable result was a more relaxed and constructive approach to the ride, a more confidence instilling approach for your horse, and a more likely opportunity for success and skill development in the moment. Horses, after all, are more likely to reattempt challenging jumping and dressage exercises when they believe that they have the best possible chance of succeeding.

Approaching your setbacks with a positive perspective, however, is not to say that you disregard why earlier setbacks happened. Many an optimistic athlete among those I have worked with tended to relearn from their mistakes time and again because they assumed that everything would work itself out. I have always argued that optimal performance is not inevitable, even for the most positive minded among us. There is often a good reason why a schooling sessions or competition experience falls short. Assuming that things will get better tomorrow without also considering how to make them better through a revised riding or exercise strategy is overly optimistic. Part of the objective while believing that things will improve is to consider how the improvement will happen. Through a systematic evaluation of why your earlier ride fell short, you will learn how to rebuild horse and rider confidence and progression. A consideration of how to improve upon earlier mistakes also provides some useful long-term lessons on how to proceed with your horse, providing you are willing to consider and learn from your earlier mistakes. Mistakes are part of the solution oriented rider's pursuit of equestrian excellence.

Criteria Two: Explaining circumstances in terms of accountability

The assignment of accountability is an interesting process when it is considered in relation to eques-

trian development. I have heard many riders at all levels explain successful rides to personal ingredients including personal physical and mental abilities. Have you ever explained a good ride to personal riding abilities and tactical decisions? You might have thought 'was I ever at my best today. I did everything right.' In psychology, we term this internal pattern of explaining a self-serving bias. In terms of riding development, it is important for the developing and elite level equestrian to explain good riding performances to factors that can be controlled personally. The dressage rider is correct in explaining personal success to an accurate dressage test, clear aids, and forward riding, for instance. The cross country rider experiencing success is also correct in highlighting a strong recent ride to an attacking strategy, clear lines of approach, and a strong upper body position, among other discipline specific important riding attributes. With explanations of good rides assigned to personally controllable factors, it is logical that good rides in the future can be approached with the very same strategies. So explaining your good performances to personal skills is useful and confidence producing.

Assigning personal accountability for a good riding performance is a double-edged sword, however. To emphasize personal accountability after a successful ride while not taking into some account the assistance of your coach, your horse, your parent, or other supportive people is a mistake. All riders do need help at different times during their development. Show jumpers and event riders sometimes require assistance with the setting-up of jumps before their classes, and before important competitions with schooling and conditioning advice, for instance. Dressage riders also need ground people to guide them through final refinements and warmups from time to time. People from all riding disciplines need personal support, at very least at the emotional level to rebound from setbacks. No one achieves success on their own, even among the best equestrians in the world! The underlying message is that good rides need to be evaluated in relation to both personal skills and the skills of crucial others who assist you with your riding development. To explain success to a combination of internal and external ingredients also highlights the most important aspects of what will be needed in the future for optimal equestrian performance. You will learn what is required in order to systematize your good rides, and at the same time, it is also worth acknowledging those who are helping you with your equestrian pursuits.

You are probably wondering how to explain your weaker rides. Typically, athletes have been known to blaim their poor performances on factors outside of their control. I have heard a wide range of external excuses. For a poor show jumping performance, riders have blamed their results on a sloppy horse, or a horse lacking in desire. I have also witnessed many a young rider accusing a coach or parent of poor guidance. I personally can recall assigning accountability to someone else while competing at the Rolex Kentucky Three-Day Event some time ago. The Rolex Kentucky Three-Day Event is one of the most prestigious international three-day events in the world, and it is widely attended by spectators and media alike. It is definitely a competition where inexperienced aspiring competitors are at their best and worst. I was warming up for the dressage phase, and my horse and I were boiling over into a foreseeable poor performance. A rough ride was inevitable, and I knew it. During those progressively heated moments, my father tried to help me calm down with a few reassuring words. Things could not have been worse, and I was angrier by the moment. As he was trying to help me, I can recall yelling at him, and saying: "Leave me alone. You're driving me crazy. You're messing up my ride." I was definitely placing the onus of responsibility elsewhere - on someone else. I am certain that most of us have placed the burden for a poor performance

◎ Blaming weaker rides on external forces may help with self-confidence but does not contribute to the evaluation of training.

elsewhere at one time or another. Can you recall ever doing so? What was the incident? How did you feel when you assigned responsibility to someone or something else? What were the short-term consequences? Were there any long-term consequences?

I am certain that you know where we are going with this discussion. Attributing negative rides to someone or something else does reduce negative personal feelings before and after a poor performance. External assignments also preserve personal beliefs such as 'I am a good rider. After all, this weak performance has nothing to do with me.' Especially in the western world, which is not to be mistaken with the discipline of western riding, assign-

◎ "Courage is an important characteristic when stretching personal limits in jumping, galloping and even when riding in wide open spaces"

ing blame outside of ourselves is a common tendency. Though the maintenance of self-confidence is important, and holding someone else responsible seems to maintain it, there has to be a more accurate and fair educational method of evaluating negative performances. When I assigned my poor dressage ride to my father, I learned little about why my warm-up was not progressing in a way that could have materialized into a better ride and a better bottom line result. The shortcoming of assigning blame outside of ourselves is the limited learning that results. As riders, we need to learn why we are falling short when we are blessed with a sub-par performance. So, when assigning accountability after a weak riding experience, consider where and when you might have fallen short. Afterward, a more promising future ride will be considered based on your recent riding experience. Also of note, as you consider your own responsibility as part of the learning process, you will be minimizing your negative feelings toward other people who are truly intending to help you. Positive thinking is meant to be even handed, constructive, and solution oriented. There is nothing wrong with accepting personal responsibility so long as there is a promising future direction to your ongoing pursuit of riding development.

Criteria Three: Explaining circumstances to one or many settings

You might be surprised to learn that in some instances, riders explain their good and bad performances by general characteristics that transcend riding altogether. A positive thinking rider might respond to a successful ride in an important competition by saying: "Why wouldn't I perwell in challenging environments." I recall working with one promising though pessimistic international equestrian who told me that she was not a co-ordinated rider because she was not a well co-ordinated person in daily life. In fact, she went on to explain that she had never been co-ordinated since childhood. Interestingly, the rider was a highly successful international level rider who was respected as an athlete by others the world over. As you can gather, riders are people, first. We all bring ourselves with us everywhere we go, including into the domain of equestrianism. The positive thinking person can carry positive characteristics such as compassion, logic, competitiveness, rational thinking, and alike into riding challenges. The negative thinking person might bring thoughts of self-doubt, a lack of trust of others including coaches, and even impatience and a poor temper. Though sport holds the ability to bring out and teach us the very best of characteristics, we tend to infuse a little bit of ourselves into the sport, for better and for worse.

Optimally speaking, I always suggest to riders that they identify the personal strengths that they can bring to riding. According to one of my academic mentors, Christopher Peterson, a psychology professor from the University of Michigan, the personal strengths that people bring to sport can include courage, optimism, sound judgment, and open-mindedness while learning. Clearly, each of these characteristics can be performance enhancing skills providing you acknowledge them as part of your personal composition, and then proceed to consider how you might use them within riding to your best advantage. Courage is an important characteristic when stretching personal limits in jumping, galloping, and even when riding in wide open spaces over unfamiliar terrain. Optimistic thinking is an asset when it comes to explaining riding accountability as you know, and also, when rebounding after a poor ride. Sound judgment is essential in equestrianism given the size and weight of a horse, as well as the inertia that it carries during exercises. It would be dangerous to attempt an exercise where you were to place your body, your confidence, and the confidence of your horse in jeopardy. Open-mindedness is important in terms of ongoing learning while watching someone else ride, and when accepting constructive criticism from your coach. All of these strengths are useful, and all can be borrowed from other areas of your life, and then brought to your equestrian activities. The key is for you to identify your personal strengths and how you use them typically, and afterward, for you to consider how best to integrate each one into riding.

Just as you can borrow characteristics from outside of equestrianism, and then transfer them effectively, you can also identify some of the unique strengths you have learned from equestrianism, and transfer them into your day to day living. After all, equestrianism is another important part of your life, and it is an opportunity to learn how to be at your best in other performance environments like school, work, and in your personal life. There are many different reasons why you are drawn to equestrianism otherwise you would not be pursuing it at this moment. More than likely, you are attracted to this sport based on some very special characteristics that it brings out in you. These characteristics might include patience, compassion, generosity, competitiveness, and a love of serenity. Take a few minutes and identify the personal strengths that you have developed through riding and horsemanship. Once you have done so, consider how you might integrate each as a permanent characteristic into your general life. Doing so will be an opportunity to take stock of your riding strengths, and hopefully, use them as day to day life skills.

⊚ "When a coach regards a sub-par performance as poorly judged and political, the rider tends to acquire the very same subjective view of judging and politics."

Learning and transferring equestrian perceptions

To complete our discussion about positive thinking, you might wonder where problem and solution oriented thinking comes from. Even ten years ago, the general belief was that we learn our interpretational styles, for better and for worse, from those who are closest to us, our earliest caregivers. The belief was that optimistic parents would produce positive thinking children, who may in turn become optimistic equestrians. A similar, though opposite rule of thumb was put forward by psychology researchers in terms of problem oriented thinkers. There was a belief that pessimistic parents would produce a sceptical child, who would in turn become a problem oriented athlete. The way of thinking that we learned in childhood was meant to indicate how we would manage adversity and learning in all aspects of our life including equestrianism. Those of us who were fortunate enough to inherit positive thinking were assumed to be quicker learners and more persistent performers in sport, business, and life. The way we explained our past and predicted our future was assumed to be predetermined, though not irreversible.

The last five years have brought some important new developments to sport research and practice, especially in the area of sport optimism. Christopher Peterson and I started dialoguing and presenting some innovative new research with international level athletes as our population of choice. We learned that people do have general ways of interpreting their successes and failures, but that we could also learn more specific interpretational styles within different parts of our life, especially in sport. It is conceivable that a problem oriented person could become a solution oriented rider, providing that riding is approached in a different and more positive way than one's typical life responses. I have met many a rider who rates as pessimistic in life and optimistic in his or her equestrian world. What I am trying to say is that your riding experiences can be a positive source of life lessons, providing you take the time to identify your constructive riding strengths, and then take some additional time working on their transferability to other parts of your life. We all respond effectively and ineffectively in life's performance settings. It is just a matter of learning when and how you respond optimally in equestrianism, and then using the very same techniques in another part of your life.

What about the equestrian who has learned a problem oriented riding approach, you might wonder? There is of course a cautionary side to this story about learning. One interesting result that I first learned during my doctoral research is that the positive oriented person can easily learn problem oriented thinking in sport, including equestrianism. Our riding interpretational styles are learned from our coaches and teammates. After interviewing a wide number of renowned Olympians, I learned and then shared with my colleagues that athletes learn how to respond to sport related adversities from the people who teach them. When a coach regards a sub-par performance as poorly judged and political, the rider tends to acquire the very same subjective view of judging and politics. If you are a coach, this small but cautionary warning needs to be regarded as a reminder regarding how best to explain performance, for your benefit, and the benefit of your riders. When riders are taught that their performance results have little or nothing to do with their efforts, the outcome is often frustration, and sometimes, a premature withdrawing from our sport. Be mindful. If you are a riding student, I suggest you continue to monitor how you explain your rides, at very least on a weekly basis. Should you happen upon an excellent though pessimistic coach, it will be the perfect opportunity for the student to become the teacher. After all, learning, the world over, is a two-way process!

Getting started

To this point in the discussion of positive thinking, we have considered how riders explain their rides, and how they should. You probably have a pretty good idea of how to go about reviewing your riding performances by now. There is no mystery regarding how to evaluate rides, but few stop to consider explaining tendencies, and how they motivate and de-motivate us as riders. Explanations are a very important part of your riding development regardless which riding discipline you have chosen, and which riding level you are currently performing at. It is well worth your time to monitor how you evaluate your daily rides. Simply purchase a notepad or journal, and review how you evaluated each ride while it was in process. Also take a few moments and consider the sorts of refinements you would like to make or maintain from one ride to the next. A regular evaluation of your interpretations will provide you with a clear idea of how you think from ride to ride, and how you ought to think in order to facilitate ongoing riding development. Start this process today!

General Tips

- Evaluate good rides and competitive performances as controllable, given ongoing efforts, personal abilities, and optimal support from your coach, family and friends.
- Evaluate sub-par rides as the result of a lack of effort. Afterward, take some time to identify how you can control against declines in performance next time.
- Monitor you, interpretational style, at very least on a weekly basis.
- From time to time, monitor the interpretations of those who are supporting you. Make sure that you are learning or maintaining a solution oriented focus.
- If you are a coach, monitor your own interpretational pattern as well as those of your students. You will be more likely to develop positive thinking and positive performances as a result.

3. Positive equestrian goals

Goal-setting is one of the most interesting and well discussed topics when people get together and speak of their achievements, both past and forthcoming. There is no topic that is more meaningful to the equestrian, when focus is placed on becoming consistently better over time. Goal-setting is a necessary part of mental preparation for every equestrian athlete and coach and every rider from the novice to the most experienced and eminent of riders sets goals, either intentionally, or unintentionally. We can't help but to be forward thinking in terms of our wishes, and afterward, forward moving. After all, riding is a sport that challenges us daily. We need to develop our skills in order to respond to each challenge. The sport of equestrianism seems to change leaders regularly, challenging us to do new and wonderful things. We also respond by challenging ourselves as riders to reach for new heights, and to stay abreast with and push on our sport. Our forward movement is a safety guard that keeps our sport interesting, and our minds stimulated.

In order to respond to our search for riding knowledge and riding development, we set goals. Can you recall the first time you contemplated riding? When you registered for your first set of lessons, you certainly set a few goals for yourself. What were they? You undoubtedly wanted to stay atop of the horse assigned for your riding lesson. You might have had a long-term

goal of riding in the countryside, or even competing. During my first few weeks of riding, I watched an elite level three-day event rider school her magnificent grey horse in dressage. The sight was awe inspiring. I wanted to do what she did, sit without moving, transmit invisible aids, and develop an effortless partnership with a beautiful and well trained competition horse! After watching that one ride, I knew that I had a long way to go. I just needed a way of getting to my objective: competitive three-day event riding. The question, I thought, was how?

We typically approach our long-term and day to day riding with objectives. It is conceivable that our objectives could be too easy or too difficult. Our objectives might also be too vague, or unclear in terms of how they are to be accomplished. When you think back to your own initial riding goals and where you are right now, you might have been successful in achieving them, and you might not have, at least not initially. Perhaps your goals changed as you started to develop an improved understanding of equestrianism, and your commitment to it. Goal-setting, as you probably learned is an ongoing source of education, an ongoing source of motivation, and sometimes, a reality check. In the sport of equestrianism, the skill of goal-setting has a lot to offer. Without the proper framework through which to develop and refine your goals, however, your evolution as a horseperson will take shape in a slow, inconsistent and sometimes frustrating way. I have met many frustrated athletes of all lev-

Think back to your initial riding goals and consider whether they have been achieved, how they have changed and how much more focussed they may now be in comparison.

ing way. I have met many frustrated athletes of all levels who suffered from unclear goal-setting strategies. Goal-setting might not be a science, but it does have some guidelines through which it can be used as an effective performance enhancement aid. Within this chapter, an overview of goal-setting guidelines will be provided. Together, we will consider why some of us reach our goals quickly, where others are slower to progress, and still others slow to a complete standstill. Goal-setting is a necessary first step in the athlete and

A Personal Anecdote

Goals are an important and telling part of every rider's development. Despite being told so from my earliest riding days onward, I never took goal-setting all that seriously until my third year as a member of the Ontario Young Riders Team. It was 1986, and I had become one of the veterans within my provincial equestrian team. Though sport psychology was not a part of the provincial team's structure at that time, my mother did experiment with it at our home facility as she pursued graduate studies, and so, I was compelled to be one of her guinea pigs. The month before the American Continental Young Riders Championship, a session about goal-setting was held with three young riders attending, myself included. All of us were my father's riding students, and all of us were readying to compete at the very same international competition. In retrospect, we were all slightly uncomfortable sharing our goals during the session. Years later, we all agreed that we had the same fears: we worried about being laughed at, and also, we did not want to declare our objectives out loud. Both of these fears are common among aspiring athletes, though we did not know it at the time.

Despite our fears, we all eventually shared our goals. One of my teammates had just qualified for her first Young Riders Team, and she was tentative regarding her likelihood of success. As a result, my teammate set an objective of completing the competition. Though finishing would have been too easy a goal for a more experienced

international competitor, she was satisfied with her objective. The competition would be her first major three-day event, and the cross country course was destined to be challenging. The second rider among us was a talented athlete from a foreign country. She was slightly more optimistic, and so, she set her objective as a top ten finish. Though the second rider was also inexperienced, she had purchased a more experienced horse. The rider believed that her inexperience was offset by her enthusiasm and her experienced equine partner. To be honest, the second rider was also a little more daring than the first. I was the most experienced competitor among the three of us, and my objective was to complete the competition with a top five result, and with it, win a Canadian Equestrian Team Scholarship during the year leading up to the 1987 Pan American Games. I believed that my expectation was also realistic given my previous year's international performance on the very same horse. Finishing among the top five competitors at the American Continental Young Riders Championships became my competitive focal point.

As all three of us approached the competition, we had clear objectives. With those objectives in mind, we all proceeded through the competition. I am not certain whether you have ever set a numerical objective in terms of productivity or competitive results for yourself before. If you have, what was your experience? Did you ever achieve exactly what you had hoped for? For the

The following section will provide you with a clear set of guidelines of how best to set your equestrian goals. Read it carefully, and consider each guideline in terms of a goal that you are currently pursuing, or one that you are preparing to pursue.

Guidelines for effective goal setting

The guidelines that each of us use for successful goal-setting will typically include one or several of the six characteristics that we are about to discuss. Goals must be

• specific;
• measurable;
• achievable;
• time-based;
• relevant; and
• balanced in terms of process and outcome objectives.

When you effectively integrate the six rules that are suggested below as they are suggested, there is no doubt that you will achieve the best possible results in your riding development.

Your riding goals must be specific

If I were to ask you whether you wanted to improve your riding, there is little doubt that you would say 'yes'. If you weren't interested in riding development, you would not be reading this book, after all! When I work with aspiring equestrians, it is always interesting to ask them what they want to achieve within our sport. Some of the riders will look me straight in the eyes, and provide a detailed explanation of what they wish to achieve. A dressage rider might explain that more bounce in both the trot and canter is the current riding objective.

three of us, a fascinating series of results fell into place. The first athlete, having set the objective of completing the competition, did just that. She finished in 21st place, and in so doing, met her objectives. The second athlete had hoped for a top ten finish, and at the end of the weekend she was not disappointed. Nor should she have been. She proceeded to finish the competition in tenth place. I finished with the very same pattern of result selection, and ended in exactly fifth position, no better, and no worse.

From the weekend's results, I have grown to learn that in equestrianism, as in many other sports, athletes often set their eyes on specific quantitative results, and do as much as is necessary to achieve their objectives. Setting numerical objectives, as we are going to discuss shortly, has its shortcomings. Personally, I achieved my objectives despite having incurred more than twenty time penalties. Without them, I would have finished in first position, and there was no reason why I could not have done so. Fifth place looked like a reasonably challenging objective before the tournament, but after the fact, it actually limited the intensity of my persistence. There is much to be learned from goals. Often, our lessons come at the expense of short-term performance constraints.

Whether your riding goals relate to enjoyment on horseback or perfection of competitive performance, they must be specific.

One of the show jumpers I recently worked with sought improved consistency from round to round during important competition weekends, especially as each weekend's classes progressed toward championship points. Though the requests of these two riders are very different in terms of what is desired, both athletes are very specific in their wishes, and so, both have painted a clear picture of where they wish to go. From a clear image of what is desired, it is far easier to move forward and develop a goal-setting plan. Additionally, the rider is far more capable of maintaining personal motivation with a very clear and concise objective. Why, you might wonder? Riders are far more likely to be motivated by clear objectives than vague ones, mostly because the riders are better able to see where they are moving to, and because they are also better able to recognize their riding developments as each unfolds. With a clear understanding of where you are going, you are more likely to persist, and you are more likely to gain confidence in the possibility that you can improve your riding skills. With knowledge comes clarity and ambition.

There are other riders who lack clarity regarding what they want to achieve. I have heard many vague goals in my time. Some riders have told me that they just want to improve. Others have said that they want to compete, but with further probing, they are unclear what sort of competitor they want to become in terms of style, attitude, level, or even discipline! Other riders among us have set riding enjoyment as their goal, but with further questioning, they appear uncertain of what sort of riding activities might provide the most enjoyment. If you are currently realizing that you have set vague goals, don't worry. You are in good company. In several of the national team and professional sport training camps that I have attended, even elite athletes have started goal-setting workshops with unclear objectives. Given the importance of goal clarity, take a few minutes and list your current riding goals and life goals on a sheet of paper. Afterward, examine each goal in terms of whether it is clearly defined. With goals that are currently somewhat general or vague, try to clarify exactly what you are looking for within the goal. Once you have clarified specific goals, you are ready to move on to step two, the development of a goal measuring system.

Your riding goals ought to be measurable

Just as the clarity of your riding goals is important, so too is their monitoring. Clear goals need to be

◎ Allocate one section of your sports performance journal
to weighing up how you have achieved your goals.

evaluated regularly to ensure that you are developing the skills you wish to develop. Riders, like most
other athletes, find it easy aspiring to a higher level
of riding expertise or competition. For those of us
who innately set clear and concise goals, it is often
far more challenging to develop a specific monitoring method. Have you ever monitored your
goals? If you have, what sort of evaluating method
did you use? If you used a monitoring method, how
often did you monitor your short-term goals? Did
you monitor each short-term goal in relation to a
longer term goal? When you evaluate your goals
systematically, you are more likely to make the
appropriate refinements. Systematic riding goal evaluations will expedite your riding development.

There are several ways to monitor your riding
goals. One of my favourites is the sport performance journal. There are many types of journals that
riders can use for performance enhancement. There
are general performance journals where you can
outline riding developments after a good and bad
day's ride. When something new is learned, it can
be written into the sport performance journal. General performance journals, though, are not exactly what we are speaking about here. Instead, I recommend that performance journals have several
sections. One section ought to be devoted to goal-
setting evaluation techniques. If you are someone
who likes to write your thoughts down as a reflec-
tive exercise, at least part of the evaluation process
could focus on the daily identifiers that mark each
training session or competition's incremental steps
forward. Every ride holds new lessons and new
successes. When a new success aligns with your

goals, it should be written down with as much detail as you can muster. It is not enough to explain that you have taken a specific step forward in your movement toward one of your riding goals. A clear step by step procedural explanation of how the progression was achieved and how it aligns needs to be documented. With a detailed understanding of your newest progressive step, and a clear understanding of how it was developed, you will be more likely to gain confidence in your evolution as a rider, and your evolution as a goal-setter.

If you prefer evaluating your goals through the use of numbers, there are other possibilities that can be integrated into the goal-setting section of your performance journal. For the aspiring competitive dressage rider, judged dressage tests would be a useful form of monitoring. With all creditable judges, there have been ongoing improvements in the standardization of marking. Judges typically can agree on the numerical assignment for each of the basic transitions, lateral movements, and elevated movements, for instance. As the rider develops experience, providing schooling sessions are well designed, there should be incremental improvements in terms of marks for each respective movement. With each movement's mark, judges often provide useful comments regarding how it can be improved upon. Together, the numerical and written evaluations can be compared over the course of several shows, or a season. Similar methods of goal monitoring can be integrated for the three-day event rider or show jumper. Both jumping disciplines can be evaluated from one ride to the next in terms of technical aspects including straightness, tactical aspects including focus and confidence, and outcome evaluators such as jumping and time penalties. Again, a combination of numerical and written self-evaluations is useful as comparison points over the course of several rides, and several series of rides. Combined, the evaluation of judging feedback, personal self-evaluation and

results can provide clear indication regarding your rate of riding development, and where you need to progress to next.

If you are a recreational rider, you can also benefit from the monitoring of your goals. Written evaluation guidelines might include personal and coaching evaluations of the riding skills that you are currently aspiring to develop or refine. Some possible evaluation points could vary from the ongoing development of any sought after technical skills on the flat or over fences, regardless of whether you are a novice or expert recreational rider. Recreational riders, as well as competitive colleagues ought also to monitor personally the emotional and psychological aspects of riding that they wish to develop. For the impatient rider, two such goals that can be subjectively judged from 1-10 might be tolerance and patience when schooling their horse. The monitoring of patience might also include a self-evaluation of mood and the documentation of positive and negative thoughts, as well as the events that triggered them throughout a series of rides. The key thing to remember is that for our weaknesses to develop into riding strengths, it is worth monitoring personal changes in behavior, at very least twice each week. Over time, a comparison of two or three weeks' worth of self-evaluations can provide a useful indication of whether and how quickly you are moving toward your goals. When you set your goals, make sure that you evaluate their progress every few weeks.

Your riding goals ought to be achievable

There has always been debate regarding what a realistic goal truly is. I have been witness to riders surpassing and falling short of the realistic standards of their coaches and their parents. I recall watching a young twelve-year-old girl galloping by me out of control at a local combined event. I was on site

◎ Whatever your short-term goals may be, make sure that your continue to stretch yourself in their achievement.

as a coach to a wide number of aspiring junior competitors at the time. To me, the young girl looked over-horsed, frightened, and uncoordinated. When I returned to the stabling area later in the day, I had the opportunity to meet the young competitor. To my surprise, she was undeterred. Further, I got the distinct impression that she regarded herself as highly talented. She was ambitious, and as it turned out, she was persistent. Her parents paired her with an experienced though underrated horse. Four years later, Caro Angus won a medal at the Canadian Young Riders Championships. Three years later, again, she became the youngest Canadian Equestrian Team Member at the Barcelona Olympic Games, on a horse that others had no confidence in. I have learned that there are many different views regarding what can truly be achieved by each one of us. The best long-term judge of goal realism is you, the rider.

You need to be optimistic about what you can achieve in order for you to pursue whatever you truly desire. Without positive thinking, you will be hard pressed to consider long-term objectives that require colour as opposed to black and white conservatism. In the short-term however, your goal-setting practices need to be achievable. Each short-term goal should be a healthy and slightly uncomfortable stretch for you. If you are not slightly uncomfortable with your objectives as you are striving to meet each one, it is highly possible that your goals are too easy. Easily achieved goals are useful when riders lack confidence, though only for a short period of time. Afterward, riders need to push forward with modest amounts of challenge. Challenges are healthy, don't shy away from them. As you strive, push toward and achieve slightly uncomfortable goals, you will notice a personal gain in confidence. Goal-setting is a skill, and you need to work your

◎ Identify where you would like to be in four years time and then consider how you are going to progress that development for each of the years in between.

desires like you would a body muscle. As you stretch muscles, there is a resistance point that you are meant to hold until your muscle relaxes and gives. After a few stretching sessions, the resistance point is experienced a little bit further into the stretch. Applying the notion of stretching to goals, with the accomplishment of smaller successes, you, in conjunction with your coach, can develop a progressively more daring course map. The main key to any achievable goal is logical progression. Consider an equestrian short-term goal that you have been working on during this chapter. Is it achievable? If your goal is achievable, is it too easily met? Make sure that you are stretching yourself during the goal. If you are not, rework your goal until it is a slightly more challenging objective.

Your riding goals ought to be time based

As a child, I will bet that someone bought you a draw by numbers sketching book. Can you recall joining a whole bunch of numbers until a picture developed? What an amazing experience! A page filled with numbers probably made absolutely no sense to you until you put pencil to paper, and worked your way through the exercise and around the paper in a clockwise way. Goal-setting works in much the same way as a draw by numbers sketching book. The clearest drawing happens when you join the numbers chronologically from low to high. If you were to start your sketch with the largest number and work your way downward from the end point of the drawing to the beginning point,

◎ All too frequently riders lose sight of their original goals - recreational riders become nervous competitors, for example.

we face as equestrians, we are obviously pursuing our rides with some sort of long-term objective in mind. What is yours? Take a few minutes and consider the long-term [four year] objective that you are currently pursuing. Once you have done so, read on.

Your long-term objective will vary depending on time constraints, interest, coaching and financial resources, access to a training venue, and the horse you have selected, among other considerations. Now that you know where you want to go with your riding, how do you intend to get there? Where do you need to be in year one, year two, and year three, in order to arrive successfully at your longer-term goal by year four? Take as long as you need to consider where you need to be in terms of development for each of the next three years to arrive at your final destination by year four. What you are doing as you explore what I like to call "mid-range timelines", is developing the rough outline for your goal-setting sketch. The general direction of your four year goal is starting to make a little sense in terms of general overview. Now it is time to get down to the details. I always tell the athletes I work with that "success is in the details".

you would be following a process similar to a time based goal-setting exercise. Typically, I always suggest that athletes start with an objective that is four years into the future. I would ask the rider or coach: "Where do you want to be in four years from now as an equestrian?" Some riders respond with a confused look, and say: "What do you mean?" Riding requires a lot of motivation. It requires time to drive out to the barn, time to groom and get to know your horse, time to warm up, time to ride, time to cool your horse down, and time to drive home. All of these time constraints don't even include the mental preparation and planning required for progressive riding or coaching! Given the demands that

Your riding goals ought to be meaningful to you

Over the years that I have ridden, coached, and consulted, there have been countless times when riders somehow landed up pursuing goals that were unimportant to them. Recreational adult riders who truly wanted to ride as a form of relaxation and release landed up as nervous and overwhelmed competitors. Keen junior competitors with a love of dressage ended up as scared jumping and three-day event competitors. Talented and committed aspiring riders found themselves pursuing recreational riding objectives. All three of these examples reflect only a few riding pursuits that ended in a distancing from the horse world, and a loss of supporters of the horse industry. Have you never seen a rider who looked unhappy with his or her current riding status? More times than not, if you were to follow unhappy riders for a period of time, you would find that their unhappiness is somehow linked to riding pursuits that are personally meaningless. In the world of equestrianism, as in all sport disciplines, happiness stems from doing what you love.

You are probably wondering how riders lose their course, and end up pursuing a dream that is not truly their own? Just as we all have witnessed doctors who became doctors for reasons other than personal satisfaction, riders sometimes follow the dreams and hopes of their supporting cast. We all enjoy some recognition from the important people who surround us. When recognition is provided for a riding task other than the one we hold as important, we sometimes end up pursuing someone else's goals. Coaches, parents and friends all mean the very best when providing their support. In terms of goal-setting, though, the only future that truly holds meaning for all riders is their own hopes and dreams. As you are setting and evaluating your goals, you need to constantly ask yourself whether the goals you are pursuing are your own. If you find that your pursuits are truly what you desire, then you are on the right track! If you find that your goals are not as meaningful as other potential riding pursuits, consider what you truly want to do with you riding, and pursue it to the endth degree. Don't worry about pleasing others. Truly, your supporting cast will be happiest when they see you satisfied and motivated by the sport you were initially attracted to: riding. It is important that you align your goals with you own hopes and dreams. That way, you will be sure to continue in a sport that we both hold dear. Take the time necessary, and make certain that you have complete ownership over the goals you have chosen to follow and reach for.

Your riding goals ought to include process and outcome aspects

During an earlier section of this chapter, I confessed that two of my teammates and I sold ourselves short at an international Young Riders Championship through outcome oriented thinking. We each aspired to specific numerical results, and we achieved what we aspired to. The results we hoped for were not necessarily as ambitious as they could have been. Did anything go wrong with our goal-setting exercise? The feeling of achieving what you hope for, only to realize that you were capable of better is a bitter sweet feeling. Have you ever achieved what you hoped for as a rider, only to realize that you could have excelled further? How did you feel about that specific riding performance? Were you happy? You were probably not entirely happy with the result, especially after you started processing through the experience. Were you satisfied? Again, you probably sensed that the ride was somewhat incomplete. I recall James Wofford, a world renowned three-day event rider and coach explaining riding performance as a crucible, with the complete performance leaving no residue. It seemed that all three of us did not fully integrate our capabilities during the competition. Considering the experience in hindsight, our overly conservative numerical goals contributed to feelings of guilt. Pushing a step further, under-achieved performance generally robs performers from the best ever results that end in positive memories and increased confidence.

It seems that focusing on numerical evaluators like ribbons are not a complete solution if your goal is riding at your best. After all, how could it be, given that numerical results are based on the opinion of other people? Outcome goals aren't fully within your control, even though there are actions you can take to make them more likely. If an emphasis on bottom line results is not the answer to full

 If you dream of a ride through an enchanted forest, keep your objective in mind and don't pursue aspects of riding that will be counter productive.

riding potential, then surely, taking a process oriented approach must be the key. Focusing on process implies that you set goals emphasizing riding development over numerical results. Examples of process goals include being softer during a dressage ride, being more aggressive or courageous on the cross country course, and cutting more corners or leaving out more strides in a jump-off competition. For daily rides, a process orientation could also include being more positive with your horse, being more systematic with your warm-up, and even taking the time to enjoy your ride! You get the picture. Process oriented goals are more about the journey, than the destination. When you consider the process aspect of your ride, your focus is typically in this moment, on this ride, and what you can do to make it better and more enjoyable. As you work on your riding development, process oriented goals are useful because they help you emphasize the aspects of your ride that you can control: your attitude, your riding plan, and your rapport with your horse and your coach, for instance.

As you can see, the discussion about outcome and process oriented goals, and how they mix into the complete performance is an interesting one. Outcome oriented goals do motivate us to push forward and strive for tangible results. The equestrian coach who strives to produce an Olympic Gold Medal rider is motivated in part by 'the brass ring'. To develop an Olympic Champion or any major games champion for that matter, the coach must teach perspective, composure, courage, and persistence. Riding development for all riders is not entirely about bottom line results. So, to develop in your riding, you need to strike a balance between the ride and where it can take you. The balance you establish needs to be suited to the type of equestrian you want to be, and the type of life you have chosen to lead.

If you are a serious competitive rider who tends to get nervous as your competition proceeds, your balance needs to emphasize the riding process. You need to focus on your warm-up, the relationship you are building with your horse, the fluidity of your aids, your riding accuracy, and most important, your enjoyment. In addition, your process orientation could be helped through a wider perspective of riding in relation to your life.

If you ride for the sheer pleasure of riding, and your main objective is personal wellbeing, your emphasis needs to be placed most on what makes you happiest, whether it be a high intensity lesson, a methodical and low intensity training session, or a ride through an enchanted forest alone or with others. Your key objective is to de-stress, not to become a perfectionist whose riding pursuits have become counter-productive.

If you are an easy going competitive rider, and you find yourself to be overly relaxed, an emphasis on the competitive aspects of the show and some outcome oriented pressure might prove motivating. Regardless of why you are riding though, remember that the answer to your process and outcome question rests in a balance, not an extreme.

Take a few minutes and consider what balance you have struck between an outcome and a process orientation when it comes to your riding development. Does the balance you have developed work well for you? If not, re-work your balance until it offers you the best directives for your riding pursuits. Afterward, read the final section of Chapter Four, where you can put a few goal-setting exercises into play.

Goal setting applications

By now, you are getting a pretty good idea of the guidelines that you need for effective goal-setting. If I were to ask you to list the "do's" and "don'ts" of equestrian goal-setting, you would be able to refer back to your own refined goals. Now, it is time to press your knowledge into action. Though you can find a wide variety of goal-setting exercises in any sport psychology or motivational book, here are a few of the exercises that have been effective with my equestrian athletes and coaches: scripting, daily affirmations and journal monitoring.

Your four-year script

When you read through any of the motivational stories shared by Olympic and professional athletes, their goals tend to begin early on. Olympic athletes speak of seeing themselves on the podium several years before they even qualify for their Olympic experience. Many of the professional athletes I have worked with saw themselves performing with success in front of large audiences long before they even became eligible to try out as professional athletes. The long-term views of many of the well established elite equestrians I call friends had a long-term vision of where they were going with their equestrian dreams even as novices. It is healthy to have the sorts of long-term dreams that inspire you to pursue your deepest hopes. Future minded people push themselves forward to places others never dare consider. So what is the best and healthiest way of developing a long-term vision? Though some of the equestrians I have met emphasize their riding related goals, the best sorts of long-term visions are developed as part of a bigger life picture. I like to call these broader visions of your future, scripts.

If I were to ask you where you see yourself in terms of riding and life four years from today, what would your answer be? Just take five minutes somewhere quiet and close your eyes. Try to imagine it is exactly four years from today's date and ask yourself the following:

- What does your life look like? Describe it!
- Seeing that this book is about equestrian performance, what is your current involvement with the riding community?
- Are you still riding? If so, what is your current technical riding level?
- Are you succeeding at riding skills and activities that you didn't even attempt four years ago?
- Is your riding philosophy what it once was, or has something changed?
- How important is riding to you?
- Do you currently value new aspects within your riding pursuits?
- How does riding fit within your daily life?
- Are there any skills you have brought to riding from other aspects of your life? Are there any useful skills that you learned in riding that you are currently integrating elsewhere?
- How does riding balance with other aspects of your life including your personal life, your professional life, or both of these life aspects at the same time?

The answers to each of the questions that you have just considered is meant to provide you with some suggestion about the aspects of riding and

◎ Scripting helps you establish where you will be both in equestrian and life-style terms in a set period of time. This idea can then be used as a daily affirmation of your progress and development.

life that you might want to pursue, and how you might want to pursue them. Scripting questions are as much about your evolving philosophy as anything else, including skill development. Write out the scripting questions I have provided, and fill in an answer to each one. Afterward, take a few moments and reflect back over your responses. Are you happy with your answer to each of the questions? If not, change those you are unhappy with to more personally pleasing answers. Now comes your homework: each morning wake up five minutes earlier than you currently do, and review your four year script. Afterward, notice how starting your day with a positive and future minded riding focus directs you to a higher and more positive level of energy than you would otherwise experience. It is always good to start your morning off on the right side of the bed by thinking of your favorite pursuit: Riding!

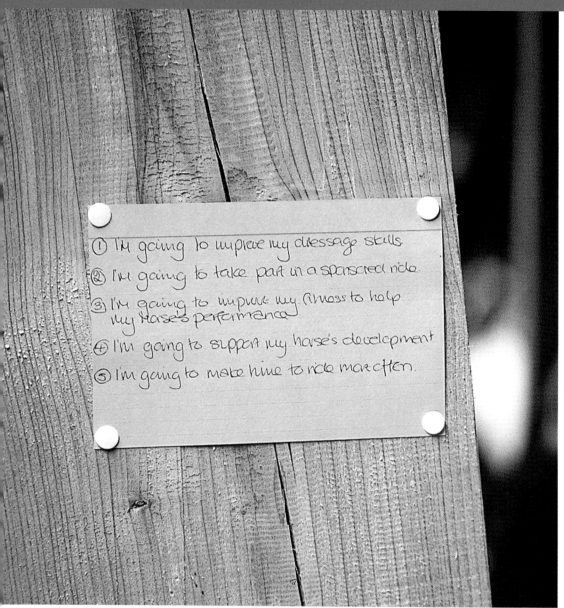

1. I'm going to improve my dressage skills
2. I'm going to take part in a sponsored ride.
3. I'm going to improve my fitness to help my horse's performance
4. I'm going to support my horse's development
5. I'm going to make time to ride more often.

◎ Tape five affirmation cards in locations at which you will see them on a daily basis.

General affirmations

There is more to goal-setting than a long-term vision. Earlier we discussed daily goals, and how each one could be refined through five goal-setting guidelines. Now it is time for you to put pen to paper, and develop a balance of four-five goals for this year, some emphasizing outcome, others emphasizing process. There should be at least two equestrian goals placed among your five goals. As you are working on each goal, remember that it should be specific, somewhat challenging, achievable, and time based. Don't be surprised if you take more than just a few minutes to consider what you want to achieve this coming year. Be patient. Do not rush the process. Once you've finished working on your five goals, read each one through carefully, check it for accurate wording, and refine it until you are satisfied. Afterward, try to turn each of your goals into an 'I am' statement. If your goal is to develop more patience with your horse, consider exactly what improved patience means to you. One possibility might be: "I am highly supportive of my horse's development." Patience in this case might include providing a lot of positive reinforcement to your horse when things are going optimally and sub-optimally. Patience might also signify allowing your horse to make mistakes without any major consequences other than a kind, caring and thoughtful correction. Having witnessed equestrianism at its best and worst with all levels of riders, patience is a useful and gratifying goal worthy of 'I am' status for the aspiring horseperson. Turn each one of your five goals into a personalized 'I am' statement, and make sure that the wording for each holds a lot of meaning for you. Do not worry if your affirmations don't mean anything to someone else. Your understanding is all that is important within the boundaries of this exercise.

After you have completed all of your 'I am' statements, consider each one again in terms of the five goal-setting guidelines we discussed earlier. Do they all make sense still? If you are happy with all five affirmations, take them and write all four-five on seven fluorescent coloured index cards. Yellow cards are usually the ones that I hand out to the athletes and coaches I am working with. After you have listed your affirmations on each card, identify the most frequented places you go each day. Tape one of your index cards to your refrigerator. Tape another card to your work or study desk. Place a third card in your family car. Tape a fourth card to your washroom mirror. Tape a fifth card either in your tack box, or by your bridle hook if you own your own horse. Find two other places to tape your cards to. Don't be shy! You need to declare and own your goals if you really want to see them through to reality.

After you have completed your taping task, the real work begins. Each time you pass by each index card, you need to stop and read all five affirmations, and take a few seconds to think about what each one means. It is one thing to set your equestrian goals. We have all set equestrian goals in our time. How many times do you typically consider your goals? Do you consider each goal daily? If so, how many times a day do you review your goals? Be honest. Most people don't consider their goals daily. For those of us who do, few people consider their goals as often as they should. For goals to happen, you need to know where you are moving to, and you need to be reminded to take the necessary actions regularly. The more you move in the right direction, the faster your goals will come true. I find that the index exercise is a useful one because the people who use it effectively actually consider their goals more than forty times daily. Imagine that! If you truly want to be motivated, you need to stay on track. The more times you are reminded of where you are going, the more right decisions you will make, the more rewards you will experience, and the more motivated you will become. The right thinking leads to the right actions, which leads to more of the right thinking in a synergistic way. Affirmations are one of the best day to day methods to improve your riding development through positive and concentrated focus. Persist with your affirmations and you will notice some significant results within two-three weeks. Once you realize that the exercise works, follow through and reset your affirmations to ensure that you are always moving forward with your riding development.

A Personal Anecdote

One of the most significant endorsements of the affirmation exercise I experienced came early on in my consulting career. I was working with a national sport team just before the 1996 Olympics. During each of the group sessions I did throughout Canada, I requested that athletes work through the exercise I just asked you to work on. One of the aspiring athletes was among the oldest on his national team. Though the athlete was clearly a capable international competitor, he had never made an Olympic team. The athlete tried out for his national team earlier, and during all three previous attempts, failed to qualify. The Atlanta Summer Games in 1996 was the athlete's last opportunity for selection, and he was willing to try anything. I always find that desperation is a good motivational tool, provided that people are focused on the correct goals. Like you did, I had the athlete list and tape his affirmations to the most frequented places he went each day. Everywhere he turned for the three months leading up to the single Olympic Qualifier, a fluorescent yellow index card was found.

Before long, the athlete became a more positive thinker. He started seeing and believing that his focus was different than earlier attempts. He was focused, unwavering, and committed like no other athlete among his team's contenders. The athlete was positive, committed, organized, and collaborative. I was lucky enough to be present during the qualifier, where, to everyone's surprise, he won, and achieved his dream. He became an Olympian during that memorable weekend. Once the athlete achieved his objective of qualifying, he no longer sought my assistance. I heard from another of the group of athletes I continued to work with that my former client finished near the bottom at the Olympics, and that the athletes he defeated during the Olympic qualification went on to win gold and silver medals, respectively. Just as affirmations will motivate you in the short-term, you need to practise them each day, and you need to reset them to make certain that you pursue your dreams over the long-term. Long-term objectives need persistent focus and commitment, they don't just happen.

Journal monitoring

There is a third step to the goal-setting practice that I teach. I like to call it journal monitoring. Just as scripting provides a long-term vision of where you are going, and affirmations provide short-term reminders, journal monitoring provides constant tangible proof that your earlier affirmations have led you to where you currently are as a horse per-

son. Knowing where you come from is as important as knowing where you are going. If you were to only consider future movement without reflecting back and enjoying past victories, and the formulas that helped create them, you would never learn to savour the moment. Every rider needs to slow down and smell the roses. Many of the higher level talented riders I know are wonderful people. Sadly, a wide number of them have forgotten all about the accomplishments they have already achieved. I see them each time I visit or compete at an equestrian competition. Some are somewhat sad, others are uptight and nervous beyond belief, and still others are bitter. It is wonderful to accomplish your riding dreams. It is equally wonderful to acknowledge your success with earlier goals. Riding has a lot to offer you, and for you to acknowledge it, you need a past, a present and a future. I recommend that you maintain a journal of past goals, past index cards, past performances, and past lessons. Every two weeks, take ten minutes and look through your documented evolution. Allow yourself to take a special pride in what you have achieved to this point. Have you enjoyed your riding journey? Take a few moments and allow your thoughts and emotions to wash over you. Your riding development hinges on your positive feelings and thoughts gained from past experiences.

 Every rider needs to slow down and smell the roses.

Getting started

What an incredible tool we have as equestrians, and as people. We can set, pursue, and acknowledge where we are going, and where we have come from. Goal-setting is perhaps the most important mental training skill that you could possible learn as an aspiring equestrian. If you integrate the guidelines that I proposed in this chapter, remain mindful of them over the long-term, and integrate the goal-setting exercises I proposed, optimal riding experiences are yours to achieve in an expedited

manner. Don't be shy to state your goals, pursue them, tell others about them, acknowledge them to yourself, and dare to challenge yourself. Forward movement is not a conservative exercise. It requires your creativity, your heart, and your persistence. Success is yours if you dream, dare to pursue, and dare to re-evaluate. Bring your goal-setting skills to equestrianism, and consider how you can integrate your knowledge as you pursue riding excellence, and as you help others aspire to the very same objectives.

General Tips

- Make sure that your riding goals are specific, measurable, achievable, time based, relevant, and balanced in terms of process and outcome oriented content.
- Remember that to be an effective goal-setter you need to consider, the long-term, the short-term, and your past accomplishments. Being future minded alone is not enough to maintain your motivation as a rider.
- Remember to consider your goals several times daily. Most riders think about their goals from time to time, and that is not enough. The pursuit of your goals is a daily pursuit.
- If you are a coach or supportive member of an aspiring equestrian, make certain that you support your rider in his or her personal dreams. If you do, the rider is more likely to experience personal growth and riding persistence at the very same time.

4. Positive equestrian pictures

When it comes to sport performance, what we see in our mind's eye often becomes our reality. Riders imagine themselves performing at varying levels of competence while preparing for a challenging riding lesson, the night before riding a cross-country course, the moments just after a show jumping course walk, and the days leading up to a dressage competition. Have you ever noticed riders who've approached their horses with expectations of a bad ride? What happened next? How about riders who anticipate success in the midst of their rides as they are readying to jump a challenging series of obstacles? What might start as one type of ride soon turns into the rider's expected ride. It almost seems that riders have an innate ability to predict their own futures. In riding, our imagination seems to take us to the riding performances we anticipate. It is typically only a matter of time before our expectations of performance gel into a self-fulfilling prophecy, for better or for worse. As one of my colleagues at Laurentian University, Wendy Jerome, says daily to both students and faculty, what we imagine will soon become our reality.

What we imagine will soon become our reality.

Every person has an imagination, and a colourful one at that! People tend to visualize events regularly throughout each day. Most of the people I know are avid imagers. Each one of us has hopes, fears, and expectations that we visualize frequently throughout each and every day. I suppose therein is the reason why last chapter's affirmation exercise works so effectively as a motivational technique with aspiring riders and coaches. Positive affirmations stir up positive images and move us toward our most positive hopes. If we repeatedly think about and imagine positive scenarios, then we are more motivated to pursue the behaviours that lead us in the correct direction toward the correct actions, and afterward, the correct results. Further, we are more industrious in our pursuits when we see them as happening successfully sometime soon. At least a few of the positive affirmations you created during the last chapter about goals are positive pictures of where you want to go with your riding. I expect that each time you come across those performance affirmations you are picturing them and the details that surround them on some level. Considering the opposite side of the same coin, negative images sometimes chip away at our capabilities as we see ourselves struggling with a task that, potentially, could be possible. In riding, as in all other performance aspects of your life, the images that we develop and relive play an important role in our development as equestrians, whether we are riders, coaches, parents, or friends.

Learning how to image in a beneficial way requires a few skills that together help create a full and positive picture. The purpose of this chapter is threefold:

(1) to explain the thoughts and senses that form into a complete imagery package;
(2) to address the influence of mental images on your riding performance; and
(3) to provide you with a few application exercises to enhance your riding performance day to day and during competitions.

A Personal Anecdote

We all learn imagery automatically, whether we know it or not. If you are anything like me, you started using imagery with your riding performance when you started riding, and you have imaged riding scenarios ever since. I started imaging as a child while at primary school, and in fact was told that I was a daydreamer each time my report card arrived. Daydreaming soon became an asset that took me to places I had only dreamed about. My imaging ability was pushed into high gear when I started competing as a three-day event rider at a more serious level. Especially the night before cross-country,

◎ What may have begun as daydreaming can turn into an imaging skill that will help with your performance. The author, seen here competing at the Radnor Advanced three-day event, would regularly sit down before a cross-country event and go over what might happen.

when I was nervous, I would sit down in a quiet room alone and work my way technically and tactically through the cross-country course. I would see myself warming up. Then, I would see myself moving into the starting box. The horse would jitter a little, the timer would count the rider [me] down from five, and the rider and horse would be off. I would see my horse and I tackling the terrain and the obstacles one by one. When I imaged a hiccup or an awkward jump, I worked on the image until it was successful, and then continued through to the end of the course, and the finish line. My pre-cross-country ritual of picturing myself would be revisited all evening until I finally saw myself galloping with confidence, rhythm, balance, straightness, and accuracy from the start of the course to its ending. The picturing of my performance from the distance of a television-like screen became a first imaging step among a number of evolving steps that I stumbled on and refined as I practised from competition to competition, and from season to season.

As an aspiring international level Young Rider, I was an avid reader of rider biographies and national team handbooks from North America and Europe. I read about national team equestrians the world over, and I had lots of heroes. In the course of my readings, I noticed a common trend in terms of imagery use. Many of the leading equestrians, including Tad Coffin from the United States and Lucinda Green from England, supported imaging in a more involved way than I did. Coffin happened to be coaching an American Young Rider's Team during the early 1980's, and he had his successful team of riders doing many interesting cross-country balancing exercis-

es sitting on a barrel with a saddle and fastened bridle. The riders were actually practising balancing techniques in a riding position as part of the acquisition of their cross-country skills. Green, when walking a course, tended to pick up momentum as she approached her cross-country obstacles. In fact, she was seen approaching many a fence on foot in a canter rhythm. I noticed that both of these renowned Olympians were far more involved in their imaging process than I was. Something had to change in my technique. I began walking my cross-country and show jumping courses imaging that I was holding reins and framing my horse, especially as I approached obstacles. I also started picking up the desired rhythm for each respective jump or movement, until my imagery felt like a first hand riding experience. So, as part of my progression, I learned how to step into my imagery until I saw it from the rider's point of view. All I saw was the horse's neck, my reins, and what was in front of the horse and I as we approached in unison. My pre-cross-country evenings also evolved into first hand experiences. Instead of imaging my performances while lying down, which seems to be a common trend among developing riders, I started imaging from a sitting position, in a chair, or standing up depending on the discipline I was rehearsing, with my legs and body in the correct balanced position. With the development of my imagery skills, I started gathering more confidence. It seemed that the more I imaged the correct performance before competing, the more it became smooth and familiar. Imagery became a large part of my riding preparation, and the images that I practised readied me for some pretty challenging and rewarding circumstances.

⊙ Imaging can become a large part of your riding preparation.

The four aspects of mental imagery

Recently, I was asked to guest review an academic article about imagery for a renowned scientific journal. The authors incorrectly used the terms imagery and visualization interchangeably to infer the very same sport enhancement technique. When you imagine riding performances, there are a number of potential senses that you can call on, and only one is visual. The researchers mistook imagery with one of its components, visualization. As Tad Coffin and Lucinda Green recognized in their own riding and coaching practices, imagery can combine a number of different senses and techniques in the creation of the complete performance enhancing picture. Effective imaging often requires a wider number of informational sources including your thoughts, touch, posture, sight, and hearing, for instance, to create a realistic and complete imagery experience. Each of these different aspects will be considered in turn as part of a best practices imaging package for you to use.

Aspect 1: Self-talk

I have always been told that every picture says a thousand words. I tend to agree that there is a very close relationship when it comes to words and pictures. When you picture different riding experiences, and whether you can accomplish each scenario, thoughts begin to flow. If you are anything like the riders I have coached and assisted, challenging images are, for instance, paired with phrases like 'I can do it', 'how do I manage this challenge', or 'this is crazy'. Self-talk is placed on a continuum from positive and performance enhancing to negative and undermining. Words hold a privileged position in the skill of imaging. Self-talk can contribute to positive images, change neutral or negative images into manageable expectations, and change positive images into negative images. As I told a group of high-performance coaches recently in a national multi-sport workshop: "Words are powerful, and we need to pay closer attention to those we use when considering our performances." Positive images matched with kind and positive self-talk contribute to positive feelings, more persistence and more success. When your thoughts affirm personal ability, personal effort, and potentially controllable circumstances, you are imaging with thoughts and words that will lead you to performance enhancement. If you truly want to image success, it is important that you think with conviction, and use words that emphasize that conviction.

In equestrian imaging, self-talk is important for all levels of riders. It really doesn't matter who you are, and what level you are riding at. If you are a nervous novice rider who is concerned with riding outside in wide open spaces, you have probably entertained thoughts relating to the challenges of horse control. There are many distractions that can happen in the great outdoors and its accompanied wide open space. Where I live, moose, bears, deer, and partridge are daily occurrences when riding out of doors. For the nervous adult riders I know of, the inevitable and unpredictable disruptions that come with being in nature-ridden Northern Ontario, Canada, are sometimes enough to ensure a permanent retreat to indoor riding. Just the thought of a spooking, bolting, or rearing horse is sometimes enough to increase anxiety levels to a new and unbearable level. Visions of nervousness including the one I just described often come with a damaging monologue. "I won't be able to control my horse." "I can't stay in balance." "I am about to lose control." These are some of the undermining and fear provoking thoughts created to match the potentially harmful outdoor riding image. Similarly, I have known many elite equestrians who've played equally damaging self-talk as part of their pre-competition imagery. How possibly could thoughts like 'I am incapable' or 'this is impossible' foster or support positive imaging? As a rule of thumb, if you are wondering whether you undermine yourself through negative self-talk during imagery, consider whether you are short-selling your personal abilities, your effort, or the attributes of your horse.

Ok. We agree that negative self-talk is often integrated into negative imagery, where poor performances instead of strong ones are rehearsed. Performance enhancing self-talk, on the other hand, emphasizes positive images supported by positive and self-affirming phrases like 'I can handle this', 'I have what it takes, and 'I will go forward and attack',

◎ Fears of what might happen in wide open spaces are usually accompanied by negative words such as "I won't be able to control my horse."

among other solution oriented statements. Words that push you forward toward solutions are the sorts of words that hold value when it comes to improving your riding. The beginner rider needs to think about the solutions that lead to success, and support all positive images with compatible words that evoke a smile, a sense of self-belief, and persistence. Similarly, if you are a more experienced rider, or a coach of developing equestrians, you need to ensure that pre-ride images are paired with the sorts of affirming statements that lead to solutions and positive experiences, not setbacks. It doesn't matter whether you start with a positive picture and add in positive words, or whether you start with positive words, and create a more positive picture. There is no correct sequence when it comes to positive minded thoughts and pictures. All that matters is that you use both words and images together as you shift toward ongoing refinement as a horse person.

Aspect 2: Posture and touch

The link between body and mind is stronger than most athletes and coaches believe. One interesting rule of thumb you might be surprised to learn is that imaging works best when using the posture that you intend to be riding in. Some of the earliest sport psychology studies developed by my good friend and colleague Terry Orlick suggest that we tend to learn better skills and gain the most confidence when we adopt an imaging posture closest to our performance posture. If you are imaging dressage, for instance, try sitting in a chair that allows you to place your legs somewhat underneath you, and your heels in a downward yet supple position. Your upper body ought to be in an upright though relaxed position with your seat and hips as supple as possible. Emphasis should be on a straight line from your shoulder, through your seat, to your heels. Similarly, your arm position should be somewhat above your lap with your hands in front of you in a position that emphasizes short reins, a solid connection, a straight line from your hand to the horse's mouth and a forward riding emphasis. Pushed a step further, every movement, whether it be a forward or downward transition, a signal to lateral work, or a change of lead in the canter is practised most effectively with an accurate use of aid signals, delivered in correct timing, at the correct intensity. If you truly want to work on skill development or performance refinement in dressage, think out of the box and image with a posture that exemplifies realistic performance and good skill reinforcement. Similar rules of thumb apply to all other riding disciplines, be they any of the English disciplines, the western disciplines, or all forms of racing. The key is that you practise your imagery in the correct position, implementing skills with the correct timing, and with the correct amount of softness and fluidity.

You are probably thinking that imaging in a performance position sounds a little fluffy. If you have come to this conclusion, I can understand where you are coming from. After all, what sort of rider or coach would reinforce readying or practising riding without a horse? Though I was initially sceptical when it came to practising imagery in posture, I have now learned the importance of posture, and I have carried its use with elite athletes to an interesting level. Consider this: when you practise imagery, your neuromuscular system responds similarly, if not identically, when compared with first hand riding experience. The quantity of mileage you need to put on your horse, especially if you only have access to one, in order to refine each riding skill would be demanding. Much like everything else, horses are sometimes overused in terms of mileage by riders who are attempting to practise and refine their riding skills to a higher level. Oftentimes, horses are depleted and over-schooled at the expense of their aspiring riders' needs of practice. Now consider the amount of time you would need to allocate to your riding, and away from other life demands in order to nail down the skills you are trying to acquire. The time demands you would need to devote at the stables might be unrealistic, at least for now. How often have you felt frustrated by an inability to allocate sufficient time to your riding development? On both counts, effective imagery posture use reinforces the correct riding techniques and affirms them during opportune moments that you can allocate each day anywhere to practise specific riding skills. You can practise riding skills during a break in your office, at home in a quiet room, or while sitting outside on your porch! Imagery is an exercise for the opportunist in you. Practise it effectively and you will shortcut your skill development and expedite your confidence if you rehearse with the correct posture daily. As a final suggestion, when you practise the posture component during your imagery, it will be useful occasionally to ask an expert coach to watch you as you image. It sometimes happens that riders rehearse with a poor or incorrect posture, and their rehearsal reinforces an existing postural or execution flaw that also surfaces during riding, such as a dropped shoulder, a forward leg, or a hand too close to the body. Typically, and interestingly, what you rehearse provides some indication of what you will do with your body when you ride, especially in the moments when your riding is tested most! Reinforce the correct posture, and you will take a giant step forward with your riding development.

The importance of posture when it comes to improving your riding goes well beyond imaging about the ride itself. Posture can also be used as a general confidence building technique. A few weeks ago, I witnessed an important flat race. The cameras filmed the entire chronology of the memorable race from the stable area, to the jockey dressing room, mounting, and the horses being led to the gate, through to the completion of the race and the post-performance interviews. From the vantage of positive pictures, I watched each jockey walk up the steps from the stable to the dressing room, and noticed an interesting pattern. I observed some jockeys with open and confident postures. The confident jockeys seemed to look straight into and through the television cameras as if they were on a mission. Others climbed the stairs almost cautiously with slightly rounded shoulders, and a gaze that avoided the cameras, and the challenge that was to

come. My wife believed that the odds-on favourite horse and jockey would succeed in their mission, and win this most important race of their lives. I had a hunch that one of the jockeys who exuded more confidence would prevail, even though he was not the odds-on favourite that day. As the horses left the starting gate, my suspicion was confirmed. The unfocused jockey made his move to the front of the race earlier than usual as part of what seemed a desperate act, and he was unable to hold the lead in the dying few yards with the finish line in sight. Though many might consider the unfore-

◎ Positive posture that exudes conviction in one's own ability is part of the body to mind confidence building package.

seeable racing loss as astonishing and heart wrenching, it would appear that the amount of confidence portrayed by the jockey's body provided insight into his concerns and questions.

Relating the link between posture and confidence back to imagery, much can be learned from that interesting few hours of racing history. When riders, jockeys, coaches, and trainers walk with confidence, their bodies stimulate a belief of confidence, and the constructive thoughts that go along with it. Just a change in posture for the better seems to trigger positive thinking, most likely because that is how we carry ourselves typically when in a strong frame of mind. When I assist potential national team athletes including equestrians with their mental game plan before international competitions, I ensure that they approach each day of training and competition with a positive and confidence exuding posture. Straight shoulders, strong eye contact, smiles, and a walk that indicates conviction are part of the body to mind confidence building package. Rides are carried out the very same way. Imagery sessions integrate the very same confidence building posture that the riders are expected to deliver on game day. I have riders see themselves or imagine themselves first hand approaching their horses with confidence, a clear focus, and a confident posture. I encourage dressage riders to see themselves showing off as they enter straight down the centre of the dressage ring, with a posture and a facial expression that say 'look at me'. Show jumping riders are asked to view themselves as having an open posture and a smile as they walk their courses, warm-up for their classes, and enter the ring. Beginners are asked to see themselves approaching their lesson mounts with the very same open and determined confidence building posture. When positive thoughts don't come to mind during your imagery, start with a proud and confident posture. You will find that the way you see yourself acting will start a positive chain of thoughts and actions that are more likely to end in successful rides.

Aspect 3: Visualization

Sight plays a very important role when it comes to imagery. The importance of visualization is epitomized through the saying 'seeing is believing'. What we see in our mind's eye tends to add credence to all of our goals, our hopes, and our dreams. There are instances when we have yet to experience first hand a challenge that we are soon to attempt. The first ride, the first outdoor trail, the first competition, and the first Olympic Games, are all amazing first experiences that we build on as aspiring equestrians. Before ever experiencing any of the above unfamiliar moments, we can prepare with visualization. I have encouraged many an elite equestrian to surf the website of their upcoming competitions and to gain as much technical and visual information as possible for their upcoming challenges as they prepare. All of the information they gather is melded into visualization from the size of the competition arena, to its seating arrangement, to its warm-up area including its footing, to where their coaches will be based during warm-ups, to what it might look like as they enter into the competitive arena or starting box surrounded by spectators and flashing cameras. As you can see, visualization can be used as the technicolour aspect to mental preparation for athletes and their coaches.

The question becomes how can you design and practice a vision that ends in believing? If you are a novice rider, visualization can be used to prepare for riding lessons, unstructured riding practice, and outdoor rides, including trail rides. Each of these experiences, whether it be experienced for the first time, or refined into more proficient riding performance, can add to your development. The picture that you paint requires as much detailed information of where you are about to ride, what the potential challenges might be, how you are going to manage them, and what it will look like from your perspective as either rider or observer.

For the novice rider, visualization can be used to prepare for lessons, early competition and outdoor rides. Do as much research as you can to enable you to visualize every circumstance that may occur.

So, assuming that you are a novice first time trail rider for example, your visualization of an upcoming outdoor adventure can include the visual aspects of where you are about to ride, some of the typical potential visual distractions that you might encounter, how you will act and react best in relation to these environmental challenges, the optimal level of emotion that you want to bring to the ride, and the speed and vantage point that you are viewing your ride from. If you can, try to step into your visualization and rehearse it from the rider's point of view. See the horse, the trees, road, terrain, the optimal pace you will be riding at, and where accompanying riders and horses will be in relation to you and your mount. Recognize the challenges you are preparing to face, and see yourself and your mount responding in the best possible way to each typical challenge. If you want to picture a few

potential unusual circumstances such as wildlife or a bolting horse, do so with your response as optimal. Visualizing things going smoothly will reinforce automatic smooth and optimal reactions. As another of my colleagues has told me repeatedly for many years, 'preparation is key'. Visualization is an important first step when it comes to strong preparation and riding performance.

Aspect 4: Hearing

Even though you might find it truly unusual, hearing holds an important place when it comes to your riding imagery. For the cross-country and show jumping rider, as well as the race jockey, the sound of rhythmic hoof beats indicates balance and control within the rider. For the dressage rider, the sound

The sounds of your horse - hoofbeats, breathing, for example - should all be part of your visualization techniques.

International competitors learn how to manage themselves and their horses during noisy or distracting moments.

of rhythm is equally important given the emphasis on regularity of the horse's stride, straightness, cadence, and impulsion. Have you ever noticed the rhythmic sound of your horse's movement when you were having a great ride? There is clearly a unique and regular sound that develops as part of your horse's way of going. As well as the sounds made by your horse, you also omit a regular sound pattern through your breathing, your seat, and your legs during the optimal ride. If you have not noticed the sounds of a great ride, next time you are experiencing one, take the time to listen. There are telltale sounds that provide useful information about the good ride and the less than optimal ride. Once you develop an awareness of what your good rides sound like, those sounds can be used as cues integrated into your riding imagery. The familiar sound of rhythm can help you establish the right thoughts, feelings and images as you mentally prepare for a peak riding performance.

Beyond the internal sounds of your horse-rider partnership, you can also improve your riding performances by integrating a few typical distracting noises. If you are anything like me, you sometimes get distracted during work or studying by the external noises of loud music or irritated people. Have you not experienced distracting noises from time to time? It doesn't matter whether you are a recreational rider, or a competitive rider. You will encounter distracting sounds occasionally. Learning how to manage yourself and your riding experiences at best despite distracting sounds is a worthwhile pursuit. The most prepared of competitors, especially international equestrians, know how to manage themselves in relation to sounds of large cheering crowds, distracting music, and irritated people. The most successful of experienced riders have a lot to offer the rest of us in terms of learning 'what to do'. The occasional use of distracting sounds within your positive imaging will prepare you for great rides in more challenging circumstances.

Putting your imagery components to work

By now, we can agree that imagery is a useful skill set when it comes to your riding development and the creation of great rides. Together, the use of positive thoughts, feelings, pictures and sounds are meant to be blended into a complete imagery package that ends in a positive riding experience. Until now, we have considered imagery as a general performance enhancement tool. Moving forward, there are additional imagery techniques that you can try, each meant to meet specific riding needs. Generally speaking, the techniques I will leave with you as the final section of this chapter can be divided into performance and relaxation skill sets.

Performance: Using video

I love the use of videotape footage as a performance technique! I have used it to prepare all of my clients for challenging performances, and I have even used it in the pursuit of my own hopes and dreams. Sometimes, people can't develop positive riding images on their own, especially when they are attempting an unfamiliar riding skill or a thought provoking riding challenge. Others are able to create a useful and positive riding image however their image is not based on sufficient and best suited information and experience.

Video footage is useful for the beginner rider who sees other successful beginner riders enjoying their initial experiences during riding lessons. Just the knowledge that other beginners of equal expe-

◎ Video footage of early performances is a valuable building block for the novice rider.

◎ Watching video footage of inspirational riders can help with your imaging.

rience are successfully able to fight their concerns and take the giant step forward to successful riding is worth remembering. Video footage is also useful for the aspiring competitor who wants to see other more experienced successful riders negotiating like challenges. For all levels of riders, the viewing of others riding successfully at a similar level on video can provide suitable images of what to aim for.

When I was moving toward the international level in three-day eventing, I found it useful to watch video footage of two recognized American riders, Michael Plumb and Bruce Davidson. Both riders were world renowned and at the top of their game. Both had excellent strong cross-country positions, both were positive in their rides, and both served as wonderful images of exactly what to do in the heat of a challenging competition. With the correct images in mind, I would stop the video cassette machine after a challenging series of fences, and mentally rehearse the very same obstacles from the comfort of my living room couch. The video footage of success provided me with a starting point

of images when I had limited experience at the international level. From video footage to imagery, and from imagery to first hand experience, the steps of mental rehearsal provided me with a strong base of competitive knowledge that materialized into some wonderful moments at national and international levels.

You are probably wondering how to use video footage in the pursuit of your own riding? The footage I used was commercially purchased. There are excellent videos available for purchase on equestrian websites including that of my publisher, Cadmos. Educational equestrian videos are developed for all levels of riders, and can range from instructional to competitive in content. Both types of videos can provide a useful reference point to refine your riding imagery. The instructional videos will point out important informational cues that you can integrate within your performance. Videos that emphasize the experience of the ride can provide some useful images of exactly what to do during different riding circumstances from outdoor riding to elite level competing. I suggest that it is worthwhile developing an equestrian video library, and spending thirty minutes a week viewing relevant footage of successful riders riding successfully in circumstances that you are currently aspiring to. Just the picture of what to do can provide you with some understanding of the images you need to practice and eventually attempt first-hand.

Perfomance: Third-hand imagery

The emphasis to this point in our exploration of imagery practice has targeted first person rehearsal. As you know by now, first person imagery is important when it comes to developing technical 'know how'. Stepping into your riding image, and seeing it from the rider's first hand point of view, opens the door to successful experiences and successful reactions during crucial riding moments. Third-person imagery (imagining yourself perform) also serves a useful purpose when your goal is improved day to day riding performance. From a motivational standpoint, viewing yourself from the detached video screen perspective can be uplifting. As a consultant, I have always asked my elite athletes to picture themselves on the podium, or achieving the rides that end with their hopes and dreams as real experiences. It is important from time to time that riders and coaches see their end goal, and entertain the thoughts and feelings that will go along with it. Sometimes, day to day riding experiences are repetitive, and so they should be until riding skills are intuitive and ready for testing. During times of drudgery, it is useful to allow your mind to wander to the end goal - your own personal brass ring. Third-person outcome oriented imagery tends to serve as a reminder of where you are going with your riding, and why you are undergoing day to day repetition. Yes, there is an end goal, and it is worthwhile remembering it in moments when you can easily misplace your perspective. A positive riding perspective is crucial, and third-person imagery can help you re-establish it during the inevitable challenge stages of your riding evolution.

Third-person imagery also has a second use: if used correctly, it can instil confidence before you attempt challenges you are concerned about. I have asked many under confident riders to practise seeing themselves performing their respective challenges with success. Dressage riders can use third-person imagery to see themselves performing their dressage tests under a wide variety of opportunities, including large audiences, questionable footing and less than positive judges. Additionally, overwhelmed dressage competitors have used third-person imagery to see themselves completing a fluid dressage test with their relaxed, supple and attentive mount. With riders from the jumping disciplines, third-person images have assisted riders with

jumping courses that they could not initially picture themselves completing with success. I have always indicated that for the concerned equestrian, distant performance pictures could be used as a starting point and as a confidence builder that leads into first-hand imaging. So, if you can't feel and think of yourself performing a task that you truly are capable of performing, resort to a third-person image of your performance, and ensure that the image slowly develops into a visual performance with the correct pace, technique, confidence, and success. Once you have convinced yourself that you are capable of achieving the task under consideration, go ahead and step into the image as an active participant. Work from the outside inward during potential circumstances where you would otherwise land up self-handicapping and under achieving.

◎ It is useful at times to allow your mind to wander to your end goal and imagine the steps along the way.

Imagery has one last practical use, and it is very different from the performance initiatives discussed to this point. Imagery is commonly used within stress management seminars, including the ones I deliver to executives and high-performance athletes. Often-times, we use imagery to relive negative aspects of our day. I have known many an employee who relives a confrontational incident with a co-worker until negative emotions are at an all time high. Have you pictured yourself addressing an angry, undermining, or confrontational person with intense negative emotions? Though the reliving of negative incidents is not a healthy behaviour, it can offer some interesting suggestions regarding how to use images to create positive emotions and self-composure. The sort of imagery I am hinting at is something I refer to as the tranquility image. We all need to learn a trick or two regarding how to recompose ourselves and re-establish a positive perspective. The tranquility image does just that! All you have to do is identify the most comfortable of settings that you have experienced or viewed through television or magazines. The images that riders before you have identified included lying on a sandy, warm beach at sunset as the tide of the ocean ebbs and flows. Others have identified evenings in their living rooms during mid-winter, with a crackling fire, a warm drink, and a favourite book. Still others have identified trail rides and the sounds of nature as their choice relaxation image. My favourite image is a return to the swing chair that is situated on my dock at the water's edge of my lakefront property. I see myself sitting there at dusk listening to the loons, looking over to the other side of the lake, where no homes have been built, and the vegetation is lush. As you can see, the tranquility image I am asking you to consider has to be a place that is serene and special in your eyes. The location you select must be relaxing enough to lower your heart rate, settle your mind, and restore a positive perspective. Your image does not need to be similar to mine. Each person has personal preferences regarding what restores tranquility. Some of us like to relax by snoozing in a hammock, you might like to engage in cross-country skiing under the light of the moon, surrounded by glistening silver snow. Your preference doesn't need to be relevant to anyone other than you!

To develop your tranquility image, identify a location or experience that you find as the most relaxing and positive either among your first-hand experiences or in your imagination. Once you have identified the image that best suits, develop it with as much detail as you can muster. Clarify the image as if you were drawing it on a piece of paper, add colour, and as many objects as are necessary to make the subject amazingly meaningful. Next, when you have some spare time to yourself, see the image as a picture in front of you. Be patient if you don't see the complete image at first. Take a deep breath, think about what makes your image so amazing to you, and let your imagination go. During days that are particularly stressful, or during times where you feel tired and overwhelmed, lie down on your favourite couch, under your favourite tree, or in your favourite hammock. Bring a portable disk player, and listen to music that compliments the image. The music you select can be classical, new age, pop, jazz, country, or rock. Allow yourself twenty minutes minimum to explore your relaxation image as you listen to your music. If you practise your tranquil image weekly, you will be more likely to maintain patience on horseback during lessons and competitions, and you will be more likely to maintain a positive general life perspective. After all, riding starts with your perspective, and goes forward from that point.

Getting started

Now it is your time to give this book a rest. It's time to put what you know into practice. Each imagery skill set that we have discussed as part of this chapter has a unique use. Select the technique that best suits today's circumstances, and give it a try! Positive images can only help when the goal is positive thoughts, feelings, and behaviours. Once you have practised each positive imagery technique, document how it has influenced your riding. I have a sneaking suspicion that as you focus on a wider repertoire of positive images, you will increase your riding development synergistically. A fresh and positive riding perspective will create and maintain ongoing positive riding experiences, increased rapport with your horse and your sport, and obviously, more riding success and enjoyment. Give each technique an honest try several times. When a skill set works, document how you used the technique as an equestrian, the role it played in your performance, and how you integrated the technique as a step by step process within the ride. Knowing and understanding how to integrate your positive images will ensure that you paint and develop into the riding picture you are aspiring to.

General Tips

- Riding images can be positive or negative. Make certain that you image positively.
- Riding imagery works best when you integrate positive thinking, the correct body posture, positive images, and the use of constructive sounds. Practice your imagery, and gradually add all of the informational sources into your positive riding images.
- You can image in either first- or third-person. There is no incorrect vantage point. Practise first-person imaging when you are working on skill development. Integrate third-person imagery when the emphasis is either personal motivation or confidence.
- Practice your positive imagery regularly, and it will become more effective as a performance enhancing technique.
- If you are a coach, make certain that your riders are imaging detailed positive riding performances. Often-times, riders revert to negative riding images, and as a result, they undermine their own riding efforts.
- Imagery is also a beneficial performance enhancement tool for coaches and other riding supporters. Practise seeing your athletes performing successfully, and practise supporting them optimally. In addition, practise the tranquility image as a restorative exercise.

5. Riding with optimal emotional control

Emotional control is essential in the sport of equestrianism. After all, how we feel has a strong influence on how we approach horses, people and events in the riding world. There is a lot to address when we consider the importance of positive and well managed emotions in relation to good horsemanship, and within it, good riding, good horse training and good coaching. Have you ever witnessed riders losing their temper with their horses? Have you ever experienced times of impatience during your own rides? Were there days where you had infinite amounts of patience, and nothing could deter you from a great ride? If you are a coach, have you ever noticed that your emotions tend to influence how you deliver your expertise to horses and riders? In riding there is no escaping the importance of optimal emotional control when progress is the ultimate objective.

A loss of emotional control ends in sub-par riding performances, and the accumulation of undermining riding experiences for you and your horse. I always regard the aspiring horse and rider combination as a team in need of as much positive history as is humanly possible. Positive rides, which tend to follow from positive emotions, build positive memories, and increased rapport. Similarly, negative rides often stemming from negative feelings tend to build negative history, and an eroded equine partnership. After all, in dire moments, horse and rider revert back to their previous experiences and their previous habits as they decide how to respond to the current challenge. As you know, there is no better prediction of the future than the past. The past is tangible. Emotional control is the backbone of accumulated riding experiences, good horsemanship and excellence in equine performance. This is why each of us needs to fully explore the relevance of emotional control in relation to our development as equestrians.

Frustration and exasperation with sub-par performance can be expressed in many ways from losing temper with oneself, to losing temper with our horses. None are conducive to good performance.

A Personal Anecdote

Some years ago, I was invited to coach national team athletes in a foreign and remote location. The training facility included several barns, several riding arenas, a wide number of grooms, and a handful of ambitious riders. One rider in particular was interested in dressage. The rider was highly capable, and he had a highly capable horse. Together, it was hoped that the two would perform successfully in a prestigious indoor continental dressage competition. This would be the pair's first exposure to international judging, and large crowds within a confined arena. Added to the mix was a high level of expectation from a generous sponsor. There was two months separating the horse rider combination from the heavily anticipated tournament, and the rider was experiencing mounting pressure. His professional future as an equestrian depended on a good showing.

Before long, I realized that the rider habitually lost his patience with his horse. During what turned out to be regular weekly heated rides, the rider would tighten his body, and the horse would begin to worry in anticipation of what was to come. As the horse tightened in response, it began to misinterpret the rider's signals. After a few misinterpretations, the rider became increasingly frustrated, and the end result was a loss of composure, a punishing ride for both horse and rider, and several sessions of restorative rapport building and damage control. Hors-es have good memories, and when they are mismanaged, like people, they remember. Though I knew from my own riding experiences that negative emotions can deteriorate the ride to an escalating cycle of violence, there was little I could do to deter the rider from his ongoing serious losses of personal control. The coach's reasoning played no relevance to the rider as he became increasingly aggressive and impatient. The rider did feel remorse within a few hours after the completion of each undermining ride and I knew that with his remorse, there was hope for improvement and eventual success. After all, remorse indicates an understanding of right and wrong 'as well as compassion' when there is sufficient time to process through personal thought, emotions, and resulting rider decisions. The entire focus for that two month span of time leading up to his important tournament was a necessary and deliberate change in behavioural response stemming from a more positive emotional response. The rider needed to start working on an alternate response to his well-established habit of negative thinking and aggressive response outbursts. Through a deliberate athlete-endorsed intervention strategy that included changes in interpretations and responses, the end result was a continental championship, some international recognition, and more important, personal growth on the part of the rider.

Given that personal loss of emotional control is a common theme in the world of sport, and so in riding, you are probably wondering about how the rider engaged in his drastic change from intolerant to tolerant and forgiving rider. The answer to your question will be uncovered systematically in the pages of this chapter that follow.

As part of our discussion on emotional control, the main topics will include

• how to develop positive and controlled thinking;

- how to optimize your emotions through changes in body response; and
- how to identify a level of emotional control that works best for you.

Read through the pages to come, and rest assured that your persistence will be rewarded with improved skills of emotional self-control, more positive rides, and an improved horse-rider partnership.

experienced either guilt or shame after the ride was over. After all, as many riders think: 'that can't be me'. Post-ride feelings of regret are truly lessons that indicate a retrospective acceptance that you could have exerted self-control in hindsight. Yes, in riding, there are times when each one of us shakes our head, and says: "I let that ride get away from me. I am a little embarrassed. This is not going to happen tomorrow!"

How thoughts turn into emotion rich rides

I have learned that thoughts and emotions are partners in a very interesting relationship when it comes to riding performance. While thinking of people, situations, and even our own behaviours in negative or positive terms, we tend to enter into a thought process that I like to term a self-fulfilling spiral. Thoughts seem to hold a lot of power over our emotions as equestrians, as in other aspects of our life. One of the most relevant emotion refining skill sets that any performer can learn is generally referred to as resilience training. The general belief among a large group of motivational experts who teach resilience techniques the world over is that negative thoughts typically lead to negative emotions, which end in diminished control, negative performances and confidence undermining negative memories. Have you ever experienced a ride when you became critical of your own abilities and chipped away at them until they were virtually unrecognizable? You probably increased your level of frustration to the point where your thoughts were overwhelming, your emotions were negatively charged, and your body was stiff, unco-operative and unfeeling. You may have been unaware of your negative spiralling performance until it was too late, and if you were anything like me, you probably

◎ Focus on how capable you and your horse are based on previous positive experiences and you are both more than likely to produce a top notch performance.

The opposite pattern also holds true when it comes to riding. Positive thoughts tend to lead into positive emotions, and help create the most masterful of rides. Have you ever experienced a ride where you focused on how capable you and your horse are? What happened during that ride? Let me guess. You probably took a deep breath, thought of specific details from previous positive rides where you acted and reacted well in relation to your horse. You probably said to yourself: "We can do this. No sweat. We have done it before, and we will do it again today." Then you took a positive and systematic approach to your ride that was intelligible and building in positive momentum. With your thoughts, emotions and behaviours at their best, your horse probably materialized into a light, willing, and supple mount. The end result was a smooth ride with high levels of horse and rider mutual enjoyment and satisfaction. After each top notch ride, you probably knew that you were more systematic, positive and feeling. The ride, after all, was foreseeable, and it resulted from conscious decisions on your part.

Let me make this point perfectly clear: we all are capable of optimal control over our thoughts and emotions once we learn how best to foster them. Well-managed positive and constructive thoughts typically take us upward in spiral to great rides and added confidence. Poorly managed thoughts take us downward in spiral to weaker performances and afterward, a necessary pause for self-reflection and refinement. As you move up or downward in spiral, your horse will follow you. Horses can differentiate rides that are systematic and well-managed from those that lack in clear progression, patience, and positive momentum. They notice the slight nuances from one ride to the next, they know the differences in your day to day approach from pre-ride grooming onward, and they know where each general approach typically leads. Horses hold a stronger ability to remember and interpret than

many riders and coaches estimate. As a result, the approach to each horse must be conscientious, caring and consistent. Success begets success.

How negative thoughts end in negative rides

The downward spiral is a fascinating process that many riders struggle with, even as they become international calibre performers. I struggled with self-composure for many years, and believe me I am not alone in the struggle for self-control when it comes to riding performance. Riders and their coaches place a significant amount of time and resources into horse and rider development. With a great deal of devotion, it only seems reasonable that rides should build toward the standard each one of us is aspiring to. Have you never thought yourself entitled to excellent rides given the money and energy you allocate to horses? The reality is that riding experience and hours in the saddle don't necessarily amount to good rides. The skills required for consistently positive riding experiences have as much to do with thinking and emotional habits as technical expertise. Many riders and coaches focus on technical development only to realise in hindsight that positive thinking and emotional composure are lacking. The rule of thumb is simple: negative thoughts end in negative emotions and negative rides no matter the horse and rider's current technical ability. Riding knowledge is more than the ability to understand and integrate riding mechanics. Excellence in equestrianism requires self-awareness, and before that, self-reflection.

A few years ago, I competed in an FEI level dressage class. Within the class was a well regarded and gifted horse and rider combination. The rider was an Olympian, and her horse was clearly the most talented developing dressage prospect on the show ground of approximately 300 competitors. I watched the combination warm-up for their dressage test.

On occasion negative anticipation can result in a negative experience.

The rider seemed irritated throughout her warm-up, and it was only a matter of time before her horse donned the very same irritated perspective. As the warm-up proceeded, the horse began to mirror his rider, and both shared in a hostile, uptight and inaccurate ride. The horse cantered for the entire performance, and it ignored every riding signal and aid despite the depth of its training. How could such a creditable combination deliver such an inaccurate and disobedient performance, many wondered? The performance clearly started long before the horse and rider stepped into the ring. The performance, which I term a positive disintegration due to its potential as a learning opportunity, started with negative and irate thinking, and progressed onward to a weak performance routine. When we approach our rides with thoughts like 'I am not happy', 'I can't stand this horse', 'this ride is hopeless', or 'what a waste of my time', the typical end result is less commitment to the ride, less clarity in our technical delivery, and less tolerance. After all, when we think negatively, we tend to focus on and emphasize what we are doing wrong. Negative thoughts and a negative focus is always confirmed and followed up with less patience and an unforgiving approach. The unforgiving riding approach can be directed at the horse, or it can be directed internally at the rider through a negative looking glass. With both scenarios, small mistakes turn into larger confirming ones, which materialize into disappointing rides. Negative thoughts can be synergistic if we let our emotions of anger, sadness, and despair get away from us. There is no feeling worse than a loss of personal emotional control, and as you would probably agree, negative emotions often begin with avoidable negative thinking.

pel us to think forward in a process of refinement. After all, when rides are approached and followed through with positive decisions and positive actions, each one of us feels comfort followed by a sense of knowing that 'this ride is on the right track'. There is a lot of joy associated with doing what works best and ends in yet another confirming positive experience. After performance enhanced rides, where all the decisions and actions we make are forward moving and solution oriented, the personal response is typically 'this is exactly what I love about riding'. Riding provides an opportunity that few sports do. Good rides create positive experiences and physical and personal growth for two performers, not one.

The synergy of the good performance can be created by the rider through a positive upward spiral. The rider creates the positive spiral by leading in a dance that the horse is grateful to follow. Positive momentum is created through a combination of two tactics. The first tactic is an allocation of time on your part to plan the best possible ride given your horse's disposition and past experiences. Some of the questions I like to consider are the following:

(1) Am I willing and prepared to devote my entire focus to this ride?
(2) How quick a progression is best for me and my horse?
(3) What emotional approach works best for me and my horse as a combination?
(4) Is there a specific sequence of exercises that contributes to a happier and more willing equine partner?
(5) What is the end goal for today's ride?
(6) What can I do during today's ride that will help my horse and I move in a forward direction to our long-term goal?

Together, these thoughts create the necessary positive images, positive thoughts and positive emotions that will start you on the path to progression.

◎ A good riding experience presents the opportunity to reaffirm what it is that you love about riding and to use that affirmation for physical and personal growth for both you and your horse.

How positive thoughts end in positive rides

Just as riders think negative thoughts, and create negative rides, they also use the thought-emotion-behavior pathway to their benefit. As you know based on your own personal experiences, thoughts that emphasize solutions and what to do next com-

In addition, you need to make certain that the communications you have with your horse are positive and inspiring. Thoughts like 'we can do it', 'I will be patient', and 'I will take the time to notice our progressions when they happen' will provide you with some indications of how to move forward in your positive ride.

When your thoughts are focused on success before and during each ride, it is inevitable that you will experience a contagious dose of hope, positive excitement, caring, and happiness. With your ability to prepare for and carry out harmonious rides daily, you will inevitably end up devoting more time to the planning and follow through of positive rides, positive memories, and a long and exciting rapport with your partner. The synergistic upward spiral may take some effort until you fully get the

hang of it, but after a while, like all other habits, you will land up following a positive approach before and during every ride. Take ten minutes before each ride to ready your thoughts and riding philosophy. Once you feel that you have packaged a response to the pre-ride questions on page 86, commit yourself to riding decisions that only end with a positive follow through.

How to turn a negative thought into a positive ride

There are times when horses experience bad moods, riders make poor riding decisions, and circumstances are less than prefect. Let's face it, not every ride is always under our direct control. There are also

◎ Misinterpreting the comments and actions of your coach, without giving them the benefit of the doubt can lead to negative emotions that will affect your performance.

⊚ When unexpected circumstances such as a loose dog or spooking horse present themselves, question how you are interpreting the event and its possible outcome.

Whether you are a rider or a coach, you most certainly have experienced situations where occurrences needed to be reframed in a more positive way. Often times, the negative emotions that we experience as riders start as negative thoughts. Many of the less optimistic riders that I know of seem to interpret the behaviours of their coaches, administrative staff, and even their horses negatively. Misinterpreting someone or something else's intentions without allowing any benefit for doubt ends in anger, suspicion, and obviously, negative emotions and distrust. It seems that when riders and coaches focus on the poor circumstances that surround them, overwhelming feelings follow. It is a challenge to ride at your best, and the challenge of good riding is more difficult yet when you are struggling with negative thoughts and feelings. We ride at best when we are relaxed and positive partners working in harmony with our mounts, not when we play the role of adversaries.

A few years ago, while I was undergoing post-doctoral education in motivational psychology at the University of Pennsylvania, one of the tasks I was asked to complete and test was an intervention strategy to improve the interpretations and emotional responses of international calibre athletes and coaches. One of the strategies that I adapted from industry is called disputing. Disputing is a self-talk strategy that effectively can shift a rider or coach from a negative emotional state in the most challenging of circumstances to a positive and performance enhancing one. Negative spirals are started and maintained through an ongoing and increasingly negative monologue. Have you ever imagined wanting to tell someone where to go, and how to get there as a result of a thorough and negative evaluation of their behaviours? Your increased emphasis on the negative circumstance or series of circumstances probably pulled you downward to deepened negative feelings. Your negative thinking more than likely gained in momentum until a small circumstance became enormous!

Personally, when I experience negative feelings, I want to change them to something that is more constructive and uplifting almost immediately. Like most people, I do not manage anger well. There is nothing pleasant about focusing with mind, heart, and soul on a circumstance that is negative. And so, I scratch and claw my way back to positive thinking through the series of steps that are typical of disputing techniques. The first step in the process is to understand exactly what negative thoughts and emotions are being experienced in this moment. For the previously described Olympic dressage rider engaged in a negative emotional spiral, let me assure you that her performance originated from a series of split second interpretations building in momentum, and the accompanied escalating negative emotional response to each. The moment a potential circumstance arises like the spooking horse, the loose dog, or a negative person nearby, as you start becoming tense, you ought to question whether you are interpreting the circumstance in the best possible way. I have witnessed many a rider and coach scold a horse for a minor misstep interpreted as spooking. If you ever tend to interpret a specific riding circumstance too quickly and too harshly, is the circumstance truly something that always arises, or is the circumstance out of the ordinary? Does your horse always spook, for instance? Can you come up with some evidence through past memory that indicates you might be unforgiving in your interpretation? Often times, riders and coaches find themselves generalizing in a negative way about horses, people and circumstances based on limited evidence. Unforgiving interpretations end in negative emotions, negative riding decisions, downward spirals, and negative experiences. And so, you need to evaluate the accuracy of what you are thinking, all the while erring on the side of optimism, not pessimism.

How much evidence are you using when you consider a person, horse, or circumstance as problematic? The dressage rider I mentioned earlier having worked with from overseas generalized his horse's confusion as the result of belligerence. The rider's interpretation was clearly faulty given the horse's ability to perform under pressure when an approach that combined patience and compassion substituted for earlier impatience. As you begin to question your own negative thinking, you will find that a more forgiving approach leads to a quick improvement in emotions, riding experiences and rapport. By recognizing and changing a negative emotional spiral once, you can integrate improved evaluation techniques time and again. What works once can work twice! It is only a matter of identifying when you are about to embark on a negative spiral, and then evaluating your thoughts as inaccuracies. The reversal in thinking and emotional responses is a learned behaviour that needs to be practised regularly until it becomes a habit. Additionally, as you begin to learn about yourself, and the sorts of thoughts and circumstances that could potentially challenge your positive emotions, you will be able to identify a negative thought before it matures into anger and negative riding. The quicker you can change a negative emotional response to a positive one, the better.

How to work through overwhelming thoughts

When speaking of emotional control, there is clearly more to discuss than happiness and anger. In the sport of equestrianism, emotions sometimes turn to fear. Consider the first time you rode out of doors, the first time you jumped, and if you are a competitor, the first time you competed. As people encounter the unknown, they tend to respond in two general ways that psychologists like to term approach and avoidance. Approach and avoidance is closely likened to our survival instinct, with reasonable challenges ending in approach behaviours, and unreasonable challenges sometimes ending in hesitation. As we ponder whether to attempt a new and challenging task, we do so based on a calculated likelihood of success. Before tacking my horses up for my first advanced horse trials at Fair Hill, Maryland, I considered the scope of the course that was to come and whether I felt my horse and I could handle it. I believed we could, and so, I approached and tackled the course with confidence and conviction. The end result was a clear round and a designation on that day of leading foreign rider. It was my belief and conviction that translated to my mount, and so, we accumulated a positive experience and a positive memory. There is nothing better than tackling a challenge you believe as possible head on and succeeding.

Though I would like to tell you that challenges are always tackled with a positive approach, if I did so, I would be lying. As a competitor, I walked some cross-country courses that I believed would end in catastrophic performance for me and my horse. I was not alone in the occasional experience of self-questioning. Every rider experiences circumstances that are scary. I recall walking a cross-country course during an important international competition some time ago with a friend who was trying out for her country's national team. As we walked the course, my friend stopped at a two jump combination with a slightly awkward distance dividing the two obstacles. I saw no problem with the question being asked of horse and rider. My friend was

◎ Whether in competition or pleasure riding try not to prejudge a situation, such as a jump, as catastrophic and focus on the worst case scenario.

◎ Fear of accident stops many riders from pursuing their equestrian dreams.

tion being asked of horse and rider. My friend was not convinced, however. There were two days dividing us from cross-country day, and my friend spent much of her time focusing on the combination, all the while considering it problematic and dangerous. When riders and coaches label situations as impossible their feelings turn to panic or despair, and hopelessness. Though I did not know it at the time, my fellow competitor was engaged in catastrophic thinking. She was focused on the worst case scenario of poor performance, de-selection, and potential injury.

When experiencing catastrophic thought, some attempt the challenge, and others choose not to. There is more to our evaluation process of whether to approach or avoid a questionable challenge than initially meets the eye. The question of whether to push through fear and worry or not to attempt the

scenario at all requires a useful evaluation process that my colleagues at University of Pennsylvania often refer to as de-catastrophizing. Often-times, the question of whether to try a new challenge or not is based on our initial emotional response, with only the worst case scenario in mind. Each riding challenge that you face has a number of different potential outcomes that can unfold. Clearly, one of the potential outcomes that some riders and coaches focus on is termed the worst case scenario. Some beginner riders opt to go no further than the first riding lesson because of a fear of falling, and worse, the remote possibility of a more serious accident. Though the likelihood of a dire accident happening in the confines of a riding arena is relatively slim, to the fearful beginner, it can become all encompassing. De-catastrophizing is a technique I like to use in order to help fearful performers with

◎ Consider a challenge in terms of worst case scenario, best case scenario and most likely outcome and review how to tackle it accordingly.

a more thorough evaluation of several potential outcomes to the very same challenge. Sometimes, just the consideration of a number of different case scenarios tends to place concerns in their right perspective.

How many times have you fixated on a very challenging task and considered only the worst case scenario? In riding as in all other performance settings in sport, business and life, there are instances where we believe that we are about to make a fool out of ourselves, or that we are going to harm ourselves emotionally or physically. Take a minute and identify a riding circumstance where you were catastrophic in your thought. As you look at the concern in detail ask yourself whether your concern is truly logical. What truly are the chances of your worst fear coming true? Guess what, when you fixate on the worst case scenario, bad circumstances are more likely to come true than otherwise. As we discussed in the last chapter on imagery, living and reliving horrible outcomes ends in fearful riding, stiffness, inhibited thinking and yes, poor performance! With de-catastrophizing, riders and coaches are asked to describe a wider variety of outcomes including the best and most likely case scenarios. Considering a minimum of three scenarios as opposed to one is often enough to provide a healthy broadened perspective and understanding to the catastrophic equestrian. To go further, however, is even better. An evaluation of the best, worst, and most likely perspectives, with a thorough exploration of how to self-manage in relation to each one effectively is performance enhancing and enlightening.

Take a few minutes and consider a catastrophic riding scenario that you have recently experienced, and that you would like to overcome. Identify what the circumstance is, its surrounding concerns, the sorts of thoughts you have struggled with, how much time you have devoted to the worst case scenario, and its numerical likelihood of coming true from 1-100. Next, consider a best case scenario and a most likely case scenario in the same way. Describe each scenario with as much detail as you can muster. Now, describe an optimal way to manage each circumstance. What sorts of thoughts, emotions and behaviours do you need to integrate to respond optimally to each circumstance? After you have considered your concern in full detail, ask yourself whether it is still catastrophic. If not, work with your coach and develop a step-by-step plan to overcome your current challenge so that you can progress forward to the next equestrian challenge.

Applying strategic arousal techniques for a great ride

To this point our discussion about emotional control has been geared toward more positive equestrian thinking. There is no denying that in riding, positive thoughts go a long way toward great performances. Beyond the thinking skills we've discussed, there are other useful tools that you can call on to create a positive emotional climate before and during your rides. The skills I am speaking of are breathing, general body tactics, music, key words, and quick fixes.

Refining your breathing in the moment

Sometimes, the best way to refine your emotions is through changing your bodily responses. What happens to you when you become angry, impatient, overwhelmed, or nervous? Have you ever noticed that one of the first things to change is your breathing? Your breathing patterns probably alter with each one of these general responses to pressure and concern, and your change in pattern is not necessarily beneficial. As riders and coaches become nervous, even to the point of being overwhelmed, their breathing pattern typically increases. Nervous people tend to breathe more rapidly and they tend to take in less air with each breath originating superficially from the upper chest region. As breathing patterns deteriorate, so does heart rate. Nervous performers' pupils dilate, their bodies becomes restricted and tight, breathing becomes a challenge, and slowly, initially composed riders lose control over effective thought and effective action. Have you ever experienced that sort of discomfort in your body? Clarity of thought tends to wash away in a tide of nervousness and uncertainty until scattered, unclear and even frantic thought remains. Breathing can take the nervous or angry performer from composed and clear minded to overwhelmed, frustrated and panicked. It is reasonable to say that ineffective breathing can undermine a ride to the point of weakness, and even incompetence.

◎ Use DAB or deep abdominal breathing in moments of stress.

 **With oxygen comes clarity.**

Every aspiring equestrian needs to learn effective breathing, both on and off the horse. Off the horse, you need to be able to breathe deeply before ever attempting to establish a clear minded and forward moving plan. With oxygen comes clarity. I often tell nervous clients when they yawn the hour before performance that their body is signaling for more oxygen. Breathing correctly before the beginning of a performance is nothing new. Every elite dancer, actor, business person, and athlete knows how to breathe deeply and effectively before they start practising or performing. The technique that they use is often referred to as deep abdominal breathing, or DAB. Correct DAB follows a sequence starting with a slow breath inward, if possible, through the nose. When you breathing in, count evenly to four, with the number one representing one quarter of your intake, and four indicating a full to capacity breath. While doing so, push the air downward to the bottom of your stomach. Once you have completed your inhalation, hold it to a relaxed count of four. Afterward, release the breath smoothly from your mouth until your stomach becomes relaxed, and your lungs become empty. If you are nervous just before attempting a challenging test, take in and follow through on one complete breath of air. Afterward, you will be able to think more clearly, and act more decisively when challenged during your ride.

Should you have a little more time to allocate to your breathing, and you are trying to manage nerves, or to unwind after a strenuous day of work, school, or play, follow the DAB process with five consecutive inhalations. Deep abdominal breathing is meant to relax and unwind riders and coaches, and to restore clarity. If you use your breathing effectively, you will be able to manage yourself first, and the challenges that surround you second. Sometimes, positive emotional control will start with you, and move outward to the surrounding environment including the horses you ride and the people you work with.

Packaging your emotions through body posture

The importance of posture is rarely discussed in the same breath as sport psychology and performance. Have you ever looked in the mirror and felt great? What happens to your shoulders, your facial expression, and your way of moving as you tune into your inner self? Chances are that your shoulders seem to lift up in a relaxed and open posture that exudes confidence and certainty. You probably have noticed that you are smiling with a satisfied look that begins with your eyes, and moves downward through to your mouth, and lower into your shoulders and your general anatomy. As you walk away from the mirror, you are probably fluid in motion, and chances are that you know exactly what you want to do right now. During those positive moments, I will wager that you feel great!

Have you ever looked around a showground and watched competitors? If you study the competitors that surround you carefully, you will find that there is a wide variety of people signalling a diversity of thoughts and beliefs. Some people walk around the showgrounds with a proud and polished stride, and a picture that says: "I know that I am ready. Bring on the challenge!" Others among the competitors envy those around them, and think: "There is no way I am ready for this. I don't look confident like that person. How could I possibly be ready?" Confident people tend to open their bodies, and their bodies exude and establish

 Take a look around the showground and pinpoint the competitors whose posture reflects their confidence and certainty and try to emulate this attitude.

presence. In comparison, under confident performers walk without purpose, shoulders slouched and defeated; eyes downcast in a signal of resignation and self questioning. Bodies tell us a lot about what sort of performance the athlete is get-

ting ready to deliver, and more interestingly, the performer's body tells the performer what is about to transpire with her or him, personally.

So, just as you can learn from watching the postures of the people who surround you, you can also learn from your own posture, and what it is indicating about you on the day-to-day as a person and athlete. I had the opportunity to work with a brilliant strength and conditioning trainer during a four-year contract with international professional boxing. Before accepting an academic position, I travelled the world working as part of the supporting cast to a wide number of world champions. The opportunity to travel as part of the group served as an opportunity to learn from the experts who worked alongside me. Our strength and conditioning coach, Andre Kulesza, is the picture of confidence. He is tall, bright, well muscled, symmetrical in posture, visibly proud, and highly competent. Just looking at Andre leaves each client with a distinct impression of inner strength and dominance. During my four-year contract as part of the group, Andre worked with a large group of professional athletes, and he also saw it as his role to work with the management group's coaches as part of his job. The entire team had to emulate fitness and confidence. After all, athletes gain confidence by looking to support-staff who exude confidence and readiness, beyond their technical expertise.

As I began to lift weights, run more, and push myself physically, my walk changed. Many people noticed that my posture opened, and that I was more recognisable than previously. I also gained in conviction, and sensed that I had more presence than previously. It seems that Andre's suggestions were worth their weight in gold. Working on body posture takes the performer and the performer's supporting cast a long way to positive emotions and confidence. Often, changing our actions can change our thoughts, both in our own eyes, and in the eyes of those evaluating us from an external perspective. When confidence or concern resonates internally, it manifests externally. And conversely, when people start displaying confidence and stature externally, the result is increased self-confidence and persistence. Sometimes performance enhancement starts with a change of posture, and moves inward to a change in emotions and a change in thoughts. It is necessary that athletes including riders acknowledge the logical and inescapable link between mind and body.

In terms of your own riding performance, work on your posture as you approach your horse, ride and respond to all sorts of life adversity. If you are a coach, work on your posture as you approach your students. Focus daily on what your body is doing. How are you carrying yourself today? Are you opening your chest? Are you feeling tall? Are you walking with a quiet confidence that you can maintain throughout the day? When you are feeling good, take a second and notice what your body is doing. At the end of a day where you carried yourself with a larger portion of pride and confidence than usual, put pen to paper and identify as many details about what your physique looked like, what your facial expression looked like, and how you moved. After a few days of positive self-evaluation, you will have a clear understanding of the sorts of physical behaviours that you can integrate on the day-to-day as you prepare for and approach your rides. After each successful postural approach to your rides, evaluate your performance that evening. Notice how you are more confident in your riding pursuits, and how your horse responds to your increase in confidence and presence. I will wager that your horse will carry itself with more presence and dignity as you begin to do so. As your horse acquires improved self-carriage, I will also wager that its performance and willingness to co-operate will also increase. Work on your posture each day, and as a result, you and your horse will gain in stature.

◎ Select music to accompany your practice sessions that will complement your approach to the task in hand and your disposition.

Sounds and music

Sounds are truly powerful to the sport performer. A sound or a series of sounds can motivate or relax the rider, with both potential responses holding the possibility of being beneficial. To the relaxed rider, upbeat and surprising sounds can increase focus and alertness. When the rider is overly relaxed, which for some of us happens often, focus is generally broad and soft. A startling sound can ground the overly relaxed rider into the moment, in a place my colleague and friend Dr Terry Orlick refers to as 'the here and now'. In comparison, nervous riders tend to be on edge, and sudden sounds serve as warnings that lead to increased and overwhelming nervousness. To the nervous rider, startling or upbeat and loud sounds provide a highly charged level of alertness well beyond what is needed to perform with mental clarity and physical relaxation. So, to the generally nervous rider, relaxed sounds, not sud-den and loud sounds facilitate optimal focus and performance. It seems that the type, volume and regularity of sounds can influence the rider's performance in a manner inverse to day to day response patterns.

As sound plays such an intriguing role in sport performance, I always like to consider how best to use it with athletes and coaches, especially in the sport of equestrianism where learning is doubled. Music is a formation of sound that many athletes use across sports to enhance their performance. I have witnessed many a rider using portable disc players before they mount their horses. For one sea-son, I listened to Bruce Springsteen's 'Can't Start a Fire' before mounting to ride cross-country cours-es while at challenging competitions. The selection was meant to instil confidence and intensity due to its positive melody and upbeat tempo. Riders I have assisted in their pursuits have listened to all sorts of selections varying from classical music to new age, to upbeat pop and rock music. The selection we ended with in each instance was chosen based on the rider's typical disposition, the nature of riding challenge being pursued, and of course, personal preference. The riders had to like their music choice, they had to find it facilitative of complete focus, and the selections had to contribute to positive emotions.

There is no doubt that an appropriate selection of music could enhance your riding as well. Before your rides, listen to music that helps you reach an optimal level of relaxation and readiness. If you are relaxed, pick an upbeat and motivating piece of music that you really like. If you are tense, go with a more tranquil selection of instrumental or vocal music. The key is to ensure that the music you choose for each day helps you reach a state of positive emotional control and appropriate body response. You can integrate music into schooling sessions as well. When you do so, use relaxed and unobtrusive music when you are working on meticulous exercises, or when you are learning and practising new skills. If you want to use one of your rides to unwind and relax, select music that is fun and upbeat. Music is a phenomenal tool that you can resource to establish or restore appropriate focus during challenging days, before challenging rides, and during tough or casual training sessions. If you are anything like me, you have used music in the past to relax or wake yourself up. Now, it is time to systematically integrate music into your riding package as a performance enhancement tool.

The use of key words

The selection of single words holds magical implications in terms of how riders and their coaches feel, how they think, and how they respond to challenge. During chapters two and three, I acknowledged that self-talk can add to or take away from the rider's hope for success. Words that are innately motivating like 'come on', 'focus', 'move', and 'now', for instance, are meant to inspire and push riders forward to persistence and then, solutions. What sorts of key words have you used in the past as you attempted to increase your riding efforts? Have they worked? Whichever words you chose to press into action undoubtedly created an emotional response. Did your emotional response fit and move you forward to your desired objective? Words are powerful, and when they are used effectively, they can help you arrive at your intended performance destination. It is only a matter of selecting the best suited words for each circumstance.

Each one of us has a distinct pattern that we use when attempting to meet our riding challenges. Think of riders as generally placed on an arousal or nervousness continuum from very relaxed and easy going to generally tense and excitable. Where would you place yourself as a performer based on the continuum? If you are easy going, the key words that you use in the pursuit of an effective ride ought to be motivating and energizing. I have suggested to easy going riders that they select words that wake them up and focus them in the immediate moment. Words like 'now', 'wake-up', 'stay alert' and 'go for it' are a few examples that spring to mind. In comparison, I would direct the tense and excitable rider to words like 'breath', 'soften', 'easy now', and 'patience'. Once a word is chosen, it follows that it be pressed into action with progressive challenges during day to day riding for at least one week. The next logical step is to integrate the selected key word into rides during competitions of progressive importance. The intention with key word selection is to ensure that each rider transports his or her thinking and emotional response to the middle ground of the arousal continuum. It is my belief that armed with an effective key word, riders and coaches can establish appropriate positive emotional responses for every situation.

Take a few minutes and consider where you reside on the arousal continuum as an equestrian. Afterward, approach a knowledgeable riding expert who knows you well and is willing to help you with your equestrian pursuits. Together, explore whether you have an accurate understanding of where your typical emotional responses are, and where they ought to be placed on the continuum. Armed with a clear view of how you respond and how you ought to respond to riding challenges, identify at least three general categories of circumstances where you might want to call on one or a few key words. Examples might include general outside riding, challenging indoor tests, and relaxed recreational riding. For each category that you develop, identify three-four possible key words, and attempt each one during opportune riding moments, each for at least two rides. After each ride's key word use, document those that worked effectively, those that facilitated moderate improvement, and the words that were completely ineffective. With a better understanding of the key words that work best for you during your general types of circumstances, settle on one special word for each category, and integrate it during opportune moments. With key words, you will be able to develop a best suited emotional response for each riding category, and integrate it systematically until it becomes a good habit.

The quick eye fix exercise

Some years ago, I attended an international sport psychology conference for the International Society of Mental Training and Excellence. During the conference, a well regarded sport psychologist from Sweden, Dr Lars Eric Unesthal shared some of the techniques he employs working with international calibre athletes. One of the techniques he shared effectively settled his athletes and helped them return to a highly composed and positive emotional state during trying circumstance including final pre-competition preparatory minutes at starting lines during Olympic Games. Before long, many of his over aroused athletes integrated the technique and settled into focus with fully charged bodies. More often than not, the end result for his athletes was medal winning performances.

Often-times, when clients seek assistance from sport psychology consultants they do so in search of a quick fix answer. One of the typical requests is for an easy and immediate antidote to counter nervousness and negative emotional response. As a viable solution, one of the techniques that Unesthal and I now, I teach aspiring athletes is the rapid eye movement technique. Let me explain how it works. When people are relaxed, and they fall into a deep sleep, their eyes turn upward, they begin to dream, and when they are observed by sleep specialists, it is apparent that their eyes and eye lashes move rapidly. Rapid eye movement or 'REM sleep' is the body's opportunity for deep relaxation and regeneration. When brain waves are recorded during REM, there is an increase in alpha waves. After several years of life experience we all become experts in REM sleep. After all, REM is something that our bodies engage in during the deepest hours of recovery every night. REM sleep is comforting to our bodies, and it is familiar. Unesthal simply took a skill that we inadvertently practice each night, and had his athletes systematically integrate it to restore focus in their trying moments of sport performance.

With the REM technique, it is assumed that athletes can lower their arousal to a more manageable level through a response that has long been automated within each one of us. We all dream, we have all experienced a deep sleep, and our bodies have learned to associate a deep level of relaxation with the specific behaviours that we do during those hours of regeneration. The technique is simple, and you can integrate it just before you ride, or even

⊚ No matter what level of competition a rider takes part in, the use of psychological solutions to stressful competitive situations are valid.

while you are mounted because it takes no more than fifteen seconds to complete. Just relax and take a deep abdominal breath. Afterward, while positioning your chin straight ahead, let your eyes slowly look upward, and slowly allow yourself to focus on your upper eye lids as much as you can. Hold the upward gaze until your upper eye lids begin to feel heavy, and then slowly relax your focus, take a deep abdominal breath and quietly close your eyes.

If you were to try the REM technique right now, you would probably notice that you feel little difference. More than likely, you are currently sitting down and comfortable reading this book! There is truly little purpose implementing an emotional control exercise while you are relaxed. However, if you were currently nervous and faced with a challenge that is anxiety producing, that would be a different story. The REM technique is meant to be integrated solely during high arousal circumstances. Next time you are faced with an emotional challenge, and you feel nervous or frustrated, remember the REM technique and integrate it. After doing so, take a moment and notice how your body responds.

Getting started

Clearly, there is a lot to consider when your riding objective is emotional control. Positive emotional control is important to all riders and their coaches. With positive emotional control, you will be free to make the best technical and tactical riding decisions available. Your rides will become consistently positive, and the rapport you develop with your horse will be trusting. Through a consistent and positive emotional approach, your horse-rider combination will be able to manage the most challenging of riding circumstances. Both of you will be able to call on a wide package of positive and trusting memories as you both consider whether to approach or avoid riding challenges. The building blocks that you establish as your emotional foundation will lead you to a level of performance that is only possible through practice and diligence. As the adage I was always taught implies, practice does not make perfect. Perfect practice makes perfect. When it comes to equestrianism, lessons are weighted twice with two performers to be accounted for, not one. For now, work diligently on your emotional control, and work deliberately in selecting the best suited and most trusting of emotional responses in your pursuit of equestrian excellence.

General Tips

- Emotional responses can be refined with a change in thinking. Try to reframe negative interpretations in a more forgiving way, and you will reduce negative emotional responses
- Emotional responses can also be improved upon through changes in body response. By changing your posture and facial expression, for instance, you can improve upon your emotions and your thoughts. Consider what you are doing with your posture and facial expression daily as you pursue your rides.

- There are appropriate levels of anxiety and emotion for every riding related task. Develop a best practice procedure for each task with the assistance of music, key words and quick fix techniques.
- Remember that daily events, and the emotions you carry from them, can sometimes be transported to your riding pursuits. Make certain that the emotions you are approaching your horse and your ride with are best suited to riding progress.

6. Optimal learning for riders

There are many views regarding what is meant by learning. Is learning the gathering of knowledge during formal riding lessons, for instance? Some might believe that riding knowledge is transferred from competent coach to aspiring rider during crucial detailed moments of instruction. Technical instruction and competent coaching are invaluable. No doubt about it. I would dare say, however, that true learning encompasses more than just formal lessons. In terms of this chapter, true learning is tested and confirmed only when a horse and rider are placed in adverse settings and asked to react. What reactions will spring forward from horse and rider when they are tested?

Will they respond to the challenge of the moment with the correct implementation of what was taught to them? If you go to any equestrian training facility or show ground the world over, you will find that there are a wide number of potential responses for each riding circumstance, and only some of them indicate appropriate learning. Though almost every rider who is coached knows in theory how they should respond to a spooking horse, a misstep, a jumping obstacle, and the like, sometimes their responses are less than perfect. As Andy Higgins, an eminent Olympic coach from track and field and a current director of one of Canada's National Coaching Institute tells aspiring coaches and athletes, including those from equestrianism: "There is a distinct difference between knowing of and knowing." True learning indicates the assimilation of lessons daily in all sorts of circumstances, and true learning only shows itself after diligent practice. True learning is, in essence, knowledge in motion.

This chapter is not meant to cover all aspects of equestrian learning. After all, your learning as a rider or coach started long before this moment! The intention of this chapter is to uncover a number of systematic suggestions that many renowned riders and athletes integrate as part of their training opportunities. In terms of day to day equestrian learning, several aspects will be discussed as part of a more general theme that academics including my good friend and colleague Jean Coté from Queens Uni-

The true test of learning is measured by rider reaction in adverse circumstances.

versity now refer to as deliberate practice. Deliberate practice implies exactly what you probably think it implies. Deliberate practice is the diligent structuring of your optimal technical and tactical training within day to day riding. The intention through deliberate practice is to expedite your progress as an equestrian through a mindful approach. Within this chapter's discussion, we will consider how you can

- develop an optimal equestrian practice plan;
- design an appropriate training environment;
- practise the riding skill sets that you need;
- practise with a variety of optimal and less than optimal equipment; and
- train for optimal responses to riding adversities.

The learning stemming from this chapter will take you many steps forward to your riding goals, so read its content carefully, and all the while, consider how you can integrate each of the smaller discussions to your best advantage. Be deliberate!

The notion of deliberate practice

The concept of deliberate practice is nothing new to sport. Coaches and riders have always worked together to form systematic riding plans and systematic learning. Some riders tend to set their sights on recreational proficiency. Others pursue a wide variety of competition objectives. All riders, regardless of intention, share the desire to progress forward toward their goals in an efficient time frame. After all, there is nothing more intrinsically rewarding to the horse, the rider and the coach than progress. Each one of us aspires to learn and to improve regardless of whether we admit it or not.

In the search for proficiency, unfortunately, not all riders are rewarded equally. Have you not noticed that some riders progress forward on a faster time frame than others, even when both groups devote the same amount of daily time and emotional commitment to their riding pursuits? I have noticed over the years that it takes aspiring ambitious equestrians different lengths of time to reach their desired performance levels even when they are appropriately mounted and schooled. What truly separates the faster learner from the slower learner, many wonder? When I competed internationally during my late teenage years and my early twenties, some of my competitors were still in the midst of pursuing national team status despite having not achieved it with more than two decades of acquired experience at the elite level! I was always intrigued by those persistent yet slower developing competitors. They definitely had the desire to perform and achieve equestrian excellence. Most also had endless funds to purchase equipment and horses. Why did some competitors appear stuck at one level of performance results where others moved ahead so quickly? The answer to that question is partly a story of deliberate practice.

A Personal Anecdote

More than a decade ago, I chose to pursue graduate studies and so I returned to the University of Ottawa, a hotbed of sport psychology research and practice. I was able to learn from world renowned sport psychology researcher, Dr John Salmela. At the time, John was changing the direction of his research interests, and he chose to pursue the question of what elite

successful coaches do in order to help their athletes achieve international success. At the time,
there was no clear understanding why some
athletes become successful international calibre performers within a span of ten years from
the moment of introduction to their respective sports, where others are either slower in
their progress, or blocked entirely from their
desired hopes and dreams. As part of the
research team, I was granted the opportunity
to study the anecdotes of twenty-four incredible international amateur and professional
coaches. It became clear why the special coaches we interviewed in-depth produced performer after performer through carefully craft-
ed training environments. There are special
skills that each aspiring athlete must learn, and
more important, there are specific techniques
that special gifted coaches use to inspire and
teach their athletes. One common denomina-
tor shared by all of the coaches is an approach
wherein there is more to successful athlete
learning than rote practice. On a personal level,
within a two year span working with John, I
learned why I progressed forward to senior
national team status by the young age of twenty. My expedited progress to international
competitor was no accident, and it was clearly not solely a matter of physical talent. After
all, if my future abilities were judged based on
my first few years of competition results, there
would have been reason for me to change
sports entirely! There are a multitude of inter-
related reasons why some riders progress rapidly in their development, and I was exposed
to many of them. As one part of a multi-dis-
ciplinary training regime, my father, who was
my coach, would deliberately have me ride all
of the required three-day event disciplines with
saddles that were too small and inexpensive,

with poorly fitted stirrups, thin leather reins,
the softest of bits, and all kinds of clothing.
There was more to readiness than riding with
ideal equipment, I learned. A second part of
my experience included practising over timed
four foot show jumping courses with a dozen
horses in one session on hot summer days as
I helped prepare the horses for a group our of
clients, the Canadian National Pentathlon Team.
Performance in competition circumstances,
thus, was also in part a repetitive numbers
game. I came to realize that familiarity does
not breed contempt, it breeds proficiency. As
a third facet of my learning experience, during dressage tests when I practised outside, my
father would twirl umbrellas. During indoor
practices, he would invite people in to watch
my training, and as part of the process, open
and close arena doors. From the twirling
umbrellas and ever changing indoor practices
my horses and I eventually learned how to perform when faced with distractions and ongoing changes in environment. Training sessions
varied in length, sometimes with warm-ups,
sometimes without. Learning became in part
the ability to perform whether ideally or inad-
equately warmed. I also trained rain or shine
during all hours of the day from dusk to dawn.
Those distracting and varied sessions, among
a wider variety of others, I have come to realize, were all part of the grander scheme of
learning that I now suggest to aspiring coaches and their riders. Eventually, I was able to
perform any time, any place, and under any
circumstance. As I eventually realized, sometimes the purpose behind training drills is
momentarily unclear to the rider. However, it
is only with the broadest and most dynamic
of learning environments that true learning
and knowing results.

Joint understanding of what needs to be practised

Deliberate practice is a joint initiative that riders and coaches are meant to work on together. All well schooled coaches hold the ability to gain a clear understanding of what their riders aspire to. Good coaches, after all, are good listeners and good observers. A clear understanding of what needs to be achieved, however, only serves as a starting point. Coaches and riders are meant to build a path that joins the dots of progression, as I said earlier, starting from the last dot representing a long-term objective, and then proceeding backwards to the rider's present understanding and level of capability. Each dot, or developmental step, is charted with a number of accompanying more specific skills that need to be learned. Each specific skill needs to be formulated by the coach, and then explained to the rider to develop and maintain a shared inspiring vision. Focusing in further, each riding skill has to be somewhat interesting to the rider in order for it

The challenges of inappropriate equipment, intense training sessions and external distractions were all part of the training programme implemented by the author's father that contributed to his becoming the competitor he is today.

to be pursued. Far too often, coaches do have method to their madness, though their steps of progression are not entirely clear, nor enticing to aspiring riders. During moments when understanding is not shared by coach and rider, there are signs of rider frustration, decreased persistence, and slowed development. As a result, coaches also become frustrated and unmotivated by their riders.

Within each drill, then, the rider ought to understand and agree with each step of the learning process, along with its accompanying initial unfamiliarity and discomfort. After all, new and unfamiliar skills definitely push each one of us out of our preferred comfort zone. When you are faced with a lesson, or you are asked to practise a skill that makes little sense to you, go back to your coach and ask where it fits in relation to your bigger picture as a developing rider. With an improved understanding of how your present pursuit adds to your riding skill, you will be more motivated to work through its challenge and reach for the proverbial light at the end of your current tunnel.

◎ When new skills are to be learned, the environment should be simple and without distraction.

Building the necessary context

The extent to which riders learn is in part related to the environment in which it takes place. The best of coaches and their riders spend a considerable amount of time crafting optimal training environments that are well suited to momentary learning objectives. When new and unfamiliar skills are to be learned by the horse, the rider, or both at the same time, the learning environment is meant to be simplified without distraction. The best of riders and coaches initially work on unfamiliar movements in a quiet arena where the sole emphasis is to understand the day's demand, and little else. Novice riders are meant to experience new flat or jumping exercises and new skills with minimal distraction. There is enough to focus on when attempt-

ing the unfamiliar without the added dimension of peripheral challenges including over populated arenas, the presence of green horses, large audiences, and typical outdoor distractions including birds, pets, and running children. When initial learning environments are riddled with ongoing distractions, horse and rider energy becomes diffused and technical learning is diluted into a weaker formula that must include distraction control techniques. In contrast, a full task focus is preferred when new skills are being introduced. So, it is worthwhile ensuring when you are first learning a new skill that you provide yourself with the best possible opportunity to understand and successfully achieve what is being asked. Initial experiences of success in the simplest of environments will help you build the confidence and persistence necessary for graduated learning to more challenging circumstances. Once you have learned a new skill, and you are able to implement it in the comfort of an indoor arena or quiet outdoor ring, it is time to vary your learning environment, stretch your comfort zone, and make the task more challenging.

When riders and horses are unable to display the skills they have successfully learned during formal lessons while attempting to compete, or ride in other dynamic environments, setbacks are often the result of incomplete learning. The ability to jump a gymnastic sequence of fences, perform a shoulder-in, or even control a horse's gait, are all graduated skills. Riders might feel comfortable meeting new challenges in confined areas, only to struggle with them in more dynamic settings. Each skill that you learn must be learned in a systematic and progressive way from its introduction to its use in more challenging circumstances, to its eventual testing in a highly dynamic riding setting such as a competition or an unfamiliar outdoor setting. So, while mapping out each small step in your development, make certain that every skill you learn is planned in detail from beginning to final assimilation before

it is even introduced. It is all too easy to attempt unrefined skills in overly challenging settings, and in the process, experience premature setbacks. The result is often frustration, fear and slowed progression. Make your path to riding development progressive, systematic, and intuitively appealing. While doing so, work closely with your riding coach, and together, map out your progression. Ask one another what is the complete package of systematic learning steps for each skill you wish for, and follow a logical progression in learning environment complexity so that your skills are readied to surface when you most need them.

Practising the required movements

For every level of riding experience and discipline, there are specific required skills. The basic dressage rider is meant to practise a wide number of transitions when practising the basic gaits. Halt, walk, trot and canter transitions are part of the requirements that every basic level rider must learn and refine over time. In addition, basic level dressage

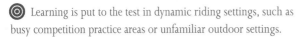 Learning is put to the test in dynamic riding settings, such as busy competition practice areas or unfamiliar outdoor settings.

tests include 20 metre circles, 10 metre circles, half circles, and rein backs, all appropriately practised with movement accuracy. For the basic cross-country rider, the ability to maintain a forward seat position, slip reins over drop fences, follow the horse's movement to the correct degree while in the air over fences, and the regulate of basic gaits on the approach to each obstacle are necessities. There are equal movement challenges for the show jumping rider, the hunter rider, all types of western riders, and racing jockeys. For each horse-rider combination, based on discipline and level, there are specific movement requirements that need to be fully learned. With the appropriate and complete riding package refined to the point of proficiency, the rider is able to tackle all the challenges that end with experienced success.

We would both probably agree that practice is an essential requirement of learning. It is easy to have coaches and riders reach consensus about what needs to be learned and integrated at each level, and within it, each smaller step of skill progression. Riders, however, do not always practise all of their required movements equally. Some riders are comfortable working on those movements needing practice. Through a complete approach to learning, where strengths are maintained, and weaknesses are addressed, the appropriately committed rider expedites personal development. However, there are others who prefer to focus on the movements that they are most comfortable with. I recall working with one international foreign three-day event rider who tried, when unmonitored, to school his horse in dressage by emphasizing their strongest gait, most of the time on the horse's more supple rein. Doing so tended to build on personal strengths, but limited the horse and rider to an incomplete set of skills on competition day. When required skills are not practised, they don't feel fluid, are slow in becoming fluid, and so, for some, they are not enjoyable. When asked to perform their weaker

◎ Whatever your discipline, the basic requirements such as slipping reins or riding perfect circles, need to be practised.

skills, such riders often dismiss their limitations with pessimism as permanent and uncontrollable. Some riders simply say: "Why bother working on skills that cannot be mastered?"

Part of your successful riding performance package is built on the awareness that you can achieve success in the most trying of circumstances. Your belief in the likelihood of success ought to eventually be founded on previous experiences in a wide number of progressive situations. When all of your necessary skills have been practised time and again to the point of comfort and proficiency, there will be good reason to put your best foot forward with conviction and persist. It is important to believe you can do the right things at the right time, but only with practice can you develop a true sense of knowing. Do not shy away from practising the uncomfortable and unrefined skills that you need right now or in the near future for a complete riding package. Know that every new skill at first is uncomfortable and unrefined. It is best to work on the widest repertoire of needed skills through each week's training plan. Set realistic short-term expectations, and reward yourself and your horse with a treat after working on unrefined and slightly uncomfortable components of your developing riding package. Before long, you will be able to stretch yourself to a new and improved level with the acquisition of new and refined abilities. You will also confirm that it is fun and healthy to explore and gain access to pertinent new building blocks. As I always say to my clients: "It is good to become comfortable with the slightly uncomfortable." For now, identify a skill that you have been shying away from, put pen to paper and write how you feel about it. Are you nervous or uncertain? Does the thought of practising the unrefined skill leave you with a feeling of discomfort? To what extent do you want to approach or avoid the unfamiliar skill? Afterward, start chipping away at the skill for two weeks. At the end of the two week period, docu-ment how you feel about the skill, and compare your more recent response with earlier pre-practice thoughts and feelings. I promise that you will experience a level of enjoyment and satisfaction from skill stretching that rewards, confirms and motivates you in your pursuit of riding excellence.

Practicing optimal thoughts and attitudes daily

Thoughts and attitudes become a habit just like any physical skill. You and I have typical attitudes and thoughts that we use as we approach and attempt to effectively build on earlier rides. Thinking habits tend to include patterns of optimism and pessimism, confidence or self-questioning, degrees of patience, levels of personal and mount expectation, and degrees of dedication. As you consider each of these facets of thinking and feeling, you most likely know best suited from poorly matched responses. Clearly, it is better to be patient when riding than impatient, and it is better to expect success than failure. Despite knowing how to approach each ride optimally, many riders are at least partially inconsistent with their thoughts and emotions. Have you not experienced weeks of training where you were more patient on some days than on others? Were there not days where you rode with more conviction? Were there also days where you were better able to focus than others? Despite knowing what works best for you, were there not times where you simply forgot to listen to your inner self, and in the process, lacked the appropriate riding strategy? The point I am trying to make is that despite knowing about what we should do from one day to the next to facilitate great rides, most of us experience occasional thought and attitude inconsistency, and the frustration that goes along with it. The consequence is often undermined confidence resulting from less positive experiences than we could have experienced.

◎ "Horses wondered with trepidation what today's approach to riding would be. Would the rider be kind and caring, or impatient and unsatisfied."

Thinking, feeling and responding skills need to be learned and practised just like all other riding skills. Riders can expedite their learning and at the same time, build rapport with their mounts through a repeated best practice approach. At global scale, popular fast food chains such as McDonalds, which is popular to the point of being considered a word in most computer software packages, you can order the same hamburger and experience the same great taste the world over! When riders and coaches train for success, they need to package themselves with the same quality control philosophy. The consistency of your day to day riding thoughts can build into good habits, and they can foster self-confidence, and confidence on the part of your mount. When both of you expect the best of performance based on your diligent self-monitoring skills, success follows.

In comparison, I have witnessed equestrians who were virtually unrecognizable in mood and approach from one day to the next, and from train-ing to competition. Inconsistency in rider approach tended to materialize into questionable horse-rider relationships. Horses wondered with trepidation what today's approach to riding would be. Would the rider be kind and caring, or impatient and unsatisfied? Considerable thought needs to be devoted to what you want to do and how you want to achieve it when working with your mount. Therefore, it is best to develop a strategy to achieve optimal thought and emotion consistency. Do you need to stop and take a few deep breaths before you approach your horse? What sort of mood and intensity do you need to bring out the best during today's ride? What is the best response in moments of difficulty or horse resistance? Take the time now to consider who you want to be on a day to day basis as a rider, and then commit to daily preparation and follow through. Quality control has as much to do with the learning and maintenance of optimal thinking and feeling as technical know how.

Fixed training times can cause competition problems. Try to vary your routine to encompass different times of the day.

Practising at the appropriate times of day

Riders, like most other athletes, often tend to schedule their rides at fixed times. University students and people with fixed jobs might schedule their rides for early evenings. Professional equestrian coaches might opt to ride first thing in the morning while they are still fresh minded. Elementary, high-school and university students typically find their way to the stable immediately after school has ended in the late afternoon. Few riders, even at the elite level, train deliberately at varying hours throughout the morning, afternoon, and evening. When training times are fixed, riders and horses grow accustomed to performing at those times. The horse and ride, practising in the early evening, for develop the ability to focus even when their bodies are slightly tired or tense. Those of us who ride in the early morning learn how to wake up quickly and focus during a time of day when most adults are drinking their first cup of coffee! The horse and rider alike can train their body and mind to pay attention at any hour of the day through regular training and the development of tactics.

Despite the positive attributes that regular learning offers in terms of predictability, comfort and scheduling, fixed times can also cause performance difficulty. When riders accustomed to late morning lessons are asked to perform at 07:00 AM for instance, the result can be an irritated horse, a groggy rider, and a sloppy performance. Have you not experienced rides at unusual times of day where you were not alert, your horse was irritated, and both of you did not fully attend to the task at hand? Riders who train at fixed times teach themselves and their mounts to perform effectively at those times. In so doing, fixed times tend to confine the horse and rider to constraining performance times with little flexibility.

Deliberate practice must include training at variable times of day. Horses must be willing and able to walk away from or hold off on daily food and still able to perform with competence. Riders must also be able to ride when hungry, tired, wide awake, and even full. Though you probably have a fixed schedule like me, try to vary your riding schedule from time to time. In so doing, you will learn a lot about yourself and your horse. Both of you need to develop a large portion of adaptability, if you haven't done so already. Further, by varying your riding times each day, you will learn how to focus and perform at all times of day. Confidence comes from a wide number of skill sets, and one of them is time versatility. Every few weeks, schedule at least one day when you can ride at an unusual time. After the ride, evaluate your performance and your horse's performance. You will gain some insight into the self-management skills that you and your horse can benefit from. Afterward, integrate schooling sessions at your weakest times of day, and in so doing, develop the necessary skills to perform at all times of day.

Training with a variety of equipment

Throughout my years as an equestrian rider and coach, I have learned that equipment plays an important part in equestrian performance. Most people will agree that it is best to ride with a good saddle, an excellent pair of riding pants, a good bridle, the appropriate bit, reins with secure grip, and perfectly fitted boots. The equipment criteria just outlined is especially important for the English rider. I have always heard that riding is a sport for kings, and despite its expense, I have always advocated for the best fitted equipment possible within the rider's budget. I still do. When the goal is to ride at your best, why not arm yourself with the best equipment? Good saddles position your legs and seat just right. A good bridle looks dashing, and riders ride best when they are beautifully presented. Reins with the best possible grip ensure that the rider doesn't have to readjust rein contact repeatedly. The perfect bit ensures the delicate balance between rider control, rider sensitivity, and horse comfort. Riding boots that provide the closest possible feel of the horse's side are also beneficial. As you can see, appropriately fitted, good quality, riding apparel is a performance enhancement tool.

Many riders are taught about the importance of good riding equipment from the start. Travel to any recognized horse show regardless of discipline, and you will find the best of riding equipment.

A Personal Anecdote

Though top quality riding equipment is a performance enhancement tool to the equestrian, I was taught by one eminent elite coach that top equipment is not as important as many of us believe. At the age of eighteen, I was fortunate enough to spend an entire winter in England with former British three-day event coach and Olympic gold medallist, Albert (Bertie) Hill. At the time, Bertie was a retired coach come gentleman farmer. He had a lot of time to spend teaching me about horsemanship. To that point, I had a rigid understanding about the importance of high quality riding apparel. I started my first training session with perfectly polished boots, clean breeches, and the typical respectful riding appearance that riders are taught as good lesson etiquette. Bertie had another lesson in mind. He looked me up and down and said: "Right, we are both going to school some young horses over cross-country fences." I saddled my assigned horse, and was surprised when I noticed Bertie already mounted. He opted to ride in soft jeans and green rubber boots, called Wellingtons. The session passed without incident. Afterward, we walked our horses out together, and I asked why he chose to ride cross-country without breeches and boots. I assumed there had to be a logical answer, and I was right! His answer was insightful. He believed that riders should be able to ride in all sorts of clothing. He asked me to consider the three-day event rider who is unable to ride cross-country with slippery reins and wet pants. Having personally experienced such rides beforehand, his response made perfect sense.

However, there are instances when even the most suitable of equipment can undermine riding performance, and wet weather is only one example. In addition, riders sometimes forget their equipment due to packing oversights, and they are left to rely on new and unfamiliar equipment during the day's ride. Also, equipment sometimes breaks. Reins break, stirrup leathers break, girths break, and breeches rip. When riders are taught to perform under the ideal circumstances, always with familiar equipment, the result is limited training, and sometimes, an unwillingness to ride in less than perfect circumstances. In contrast, the complete approach to training readies the horse and rider for unusual circumstances, which happen to include equipment problems. If you are anything like me, you have experienced broken equipment and wet clothing while riding. As it is impossible to predict equipment problems before they happen, even with scheduled maintenance, it is worthwhile practising occasionally with different saddles, and a variety of clothing, bits, reins, and loose fitting riding boots. Though you undoubtedly ride best in your own equipment it is worth learning how to ride competently in all kinds of equipment. Eventually, with practice, I learned how to ride large cross-country fences in jeans and rubber walking boots. There is something to say about being able to ride well regardless of equipment. Occasionally, after receiving clearance from your coach, alter a different piece of equipment before selected rides. Though the slight change might feel awkward and frustrating, take a minute and recognize that in the long-term you will become a more versatile rider. With versatility comes a recognition that you can ride regardless of circumstance.

◎ Competent riders learn how to manage themselves and their horses in situations that startle or excite horse and rider.

Learning to manage yourself in adversity

Many academics and experienced coaches believe that deliberate practice sessions are meant to teach the correct techniques and responses to athletes. Training sessions are intended to slowly shape the rider into a proficient performer with the correct aids, the correct balance, and the correct intensity. Within equestrianism, there are a wide number of additional skill sets that extend beyond ideal training demands in optimal settings. Training with less than ideal equipment is only one part of the equestrian's required coping skill sets. Competent riders also need to learn how to manage upset horses, and manage themselves and their mounts in situations that startle horse and rider, including riders who are out of control or unaware. In addition, every rider will eventually arrive late for a lesson, and competitors will

inevitably experience shortened warm-ups due to poor weather conditions or late arrivals caused by mechanical failure. Riding environments and riding circumstances are not always ideal. As a result, your riding education ought also to also include the development and graduated practising of self-management skills in trying moments.

In the earlier chapter about emotional control, we considered the skills of breathing, the selection of key words, and a few progressive relaxation techniques. Each one of these techniques needs to be practised during the challenging moments within each ride. When your horse spooks or missteps, when you and your horse suffer unclear communication, and when you feel upset during rides, consider each adversity as an opportunity to respond with a positive approach. There is nothing wrong with either you or your horse having a bad day or making a mistake. Other people in the riding environment must also be entitled to the same forgiving approach. Every adversity is an opportunity for you to practise breathing, re-focusing, and the testing of your positive perspective. When you are faced with trying moments at home, you will probably need to work on selecting the best suited response for the moment. It will require some thought and reflection. It may also require a time out. However, with practice, the selection of correct coping responses will become automatic and proficient. When faced with a trying circumstance, reframe it so that it becomes an opportunity and a valued testing ground for you and your horse. Challenging circumstances are an inevitable part of equestrianism, and so, you need to develop ideal responses for less than ideal moments.

The question becomes how should you integrate adversity into your day to day rides? There are some circumstances that you and your coach can develop collaboratively. Shortened warm-ups, for instance, are easy enough to create. You and your coach can also practise in crowded riding environments among beginners or green horses. There are circumstances that you can initially plan for as deliberate training sessions. Eventually, your coach will need to test your coping responses with progressively surprising circumstances. If your responses are less than ideal, coaching corrections, re-focusing and re-attempting can be integrated within the session. There will also be other spontaneous adversities that will happen on their own. We can all agree that horses and riders do have off days, and both startle, for instance. Spontaneous circumstances are opportunities to develop and refine self-management skills. The essential point that I am trying to make is that imperfect situations will happen to you and your horse. Don't retreat from adversity and confine yourself to ideal

◎ Gaining experience in busy practice arenas can be a deliberate part of your training.

training environments. Instead, regard each adversity as an opportunity to learn, and document your developing responses to challenging moments. With time you will become an expert rider with a wide repertoire of coping responses at the ready. Work on your coping skills from this point onward!

Getting started

When speaking of skill development in equestrianism, many of us consider technical advancements and graduated practice. Each rider requires specific skill sets to match with personal riding ambitions. Aspiring recreational riders seek out the necessary skills to ride with proficiency and comfort to unwind in their favoured settings. Entry level competitors within each discipline and style of riding seek out a more detailed understanding of how to press their skills into action in more pressured settings. Aspiring elite equestrians set their sights on the highest degrees of technical correctness and proficiency. Despite the inevitable difference in goals, all riders are well served by a more general understanding and acquisition of riding skill development. As an aspiring or refining competent rider, you need to consider mental composure, flexibility in training times, and equipment versatility, along with the technical aspects of your riding skill development. Riding is meant to be a broad series of skill sets well beyond the scope that many of us consider. When you take on a broadened perspective to your skill development, you will start moving toward a level of riding proficiency that is undeniably competence at its best!

General Tips

- Technical skills need to be learned based on a graduated plan. Work collaboratively with your coach, and start practising each skill within a quiet training environment. Once you are comfortable with the skill, either increase its difficulty, or add a challenging aspect to the task through environmental distractions and complexities. Eventually, a well developed riding skill can be performed at a suitably challenging level regardless of distractions.
- Practise a wide number of technical and emotional riding skill sets deliberately. With time, you will become proficient at each one, and afterward, you will be able to ride optimally in the widest number of circumstances.

- Train and practise for a wide number of perfect and imperfect riding environments. The ultimate riding goal is to ride well regardless of circumstances.
- From time to time, practise with a variety of equipment. It is worth learning how to ride well regardless of whether you are riding in your own ideal equipment or someone else's.
- Deliberate practice sessions are meant to be designed with the assistance of your riding coach. Together, you can design ingenious and enjoyable challenges that lead to your aspired-to level of proficiency.

7. Competition plans and equestrian success

Riders, especially competitors, often find their way to sport psychology as a result of performance planning needs. Putting the complete ride together on "the day" is important to many of us. It is one thing to ride well in the privacy of our own training facility, and it is an entirely other challenge to package what we've learned and put our best foot forward in pressure filled circumstances such as competitions and exhibitions. Riders and coaches often wonder why some among us are better able to package our skills on performance days in comparison to others. I have heard coaches refer to those who under-achieve as a 'backyard performer'. It seems that many of us are under the belief that riders either have the ability to perform under pressure, or they don't. Some riders appear to just don their game face at performance time, where others don't seem to have that ability. Reiner Klimke, the eminent and successful former Olympic three-day event and dressage competitor acknowledged that some riders raise their standard of performance beyond their typical response by upwards of twenty percent in competition circumstances, where others respond with under achievement. The equalizing or debilitating factor for competitive riders with equal technical proficiency is the ability to self-manage leading up to and during competition.

Despite what many equestrians think, I am going to let you in on a little secret. Every rider can withstand the pressure of performance given the desire and the skills to do so. Self-management in pressure situations is an acquired skill. It requires a 'best suited' strategy, and then, opportunity for practice and refinement. Every rider I have met over the last thirty years, whether they knew it or not, was capable of withstanding the mental challenge of performance. Some were aware and interested in learning how to self-manage, and so, they readied for and sought out competitive challenges. Others retreated, perhaps because they were not interested in competing, and perhaps due to uncertainty and discomfort. It is every rider's option to choose between riding at the recreational or competitive level. For those who are interested in competitive performance, self-questioning and discomfort are not a good enough reason to retreat. Success is built on pursuing hopes and dreams even in moments of doubt and uncertainty! This chapter is written mostly for the aspiring equestrian competitor and competition coach, though its implications are also pertinent to recreational riders who consider the term "performing" fitting to recreational pursuits such as foxhunting, exhibition riding, and displaying one's skills to friends and colleagues during opportune moments. I believe that the skills required for optimal riding performance are beneficial for the performer in each of us. Regardless of your riding interests, approach this chapter with an open mind. Don't say "I am not a performer" and then skip to the next chapter. Every rider, to an extent, is a performer. Give this chapter an honest read, and consider what it has to offer you as an equestrian and as a performer.

A Personal Anecdote

Experienced equestrian competitors develop a series of protocols that they like to refer to as their competition plan. Travel to any international competition across disciplines, and watch any elite competitor readying for performance. You will notice that there is a sequence to their day from the point of waking up onward to the culminating performance and result. Afterward, results are explained in relation to the day's events, what worked, and what didn't. Then, refinements are made, and the elite competitor re-attempts performance with a deeper sense of knowing and an increased expectation of success. As a group of competitors some years ago, the Canadian Three Day Event Team aspirants, including me, believed that we knew how to ready for competition. Our national team administrators wisely believed that we needed some refinement as competitors, and so, they hired Jack Legoff, a world renowned authority of Olympic success. As part of a widespread initiative, Legoff, the former United States Equestrian Team coach, held numerous training camps across the country, and all potential national team candidates were invited to ride in front of his watchful eye during intensive one week periods. Each day's schedule was allocated to small group riding sessions, and each evening was dedicated to theory sessions and group discussions. I approached my training camp experience with excitement. I knew that I would be exposed to a model of performance that was significantly better developed than mine. After all, Legoff previously coached countless Olympic medalists, first in his native France, and afterward, for the United States. What I learned during that one week clinic stays with me to this day as I help ready international amateur and professional athletes and coaches for optimal equestrian performance.

The complete competition package, I learned,

◉ A high standard of horse and rider presentation, as exemplified here by the author at the 1988 Rolex three-day CCI***, presents an image of success.

Self-presentation and performance

is multi-faceted. Performance readiness is a learned skill worked on with daily diligence. Jack emphasized appropriate dress at all times, and with it, an image of success. Horse presentation was held to the same high standard as rider presentation. He understood that how people look affects how they feel, and also, how others see them. Every aspect of riding and its display was part of the successful competitor's performance presentation. Performance did not start upon arrival at the competition venue. Competitions were extensions of day to day existence, and day to day habits. In addition, every riding session was a simulation that ended with at least, a partial performance routine. Riders experienced an increased pressure that became familiar, even after one week of exposure to Legoff. Dressage tests were planned on paper with precision before they were ever attempted. The argument Legoff put forward, which is now logical to me, was that precision and perfection display themselves in every aspect of preparation from accurate dressage figure drawing, to accurate dressage and jumping course walking, to accurate skill execution during the heat of battle. Performance was presented as a seamless effort with no beginning and no end. Performance is not something that the performer turns off and on. Legoff, for those who truly learned from him, was a life altering teacher and a sage. The skills he taught show themselves in my philosophy to this day as I mentor aspiring coaches, athletes and students in the skills of sport and life performance.

There is a lot to be said about self-presentation when it comes to optimal equestrian performance. I hinted earlier that how a rider or coach present goes a long way to how they feel, how they act, and the confidence they inspire in others. A spit and polished image exudes a level of confidence to the equestrian. After all, what we see in front of the mirror rarely lies! During my first winter-spring season in the southern United States, I learned that equestrians vary in how they present themselves on site while at important competitions. Some coaches, for instance, are beautifully presented. My father, for instance, always wore pressed shirt and pants, and a tie during course walks and during formal gatherings. He was not alone. Others, in contrast, wore ripped jeans, untucked shirts, and disheveled hair. Only the riders and coaches who were beautifully turned out appeared confident, and in so doing, left a distinct impression of precision, self-respect, and discipline. Their approach became synergistic among the officials, the judges, and among potential sponsors. As the saying goes, "success begets success". Those who were diligent in their self-presentation, more often than those who were not, became eminent performers mounted on high quality horses. When an opportunity for media exposure presented itself, the very same beautifully presented equestrians were asked to lend their expertise. Perception soon became reality for those who presented with diligence. To this day, you can find a wide variety of self-presentation techniques among equestrians, and only some are performance enhancing.

So what does self-presentation have to do with your riding, you probably wonder? When you dress for success, ongoing improvement typically follows. When you dress for success, you will feel great, your posture will improve, your conviction while riding will improve, and others will reinforce those positive feelings. The time allocated for optimal self-presentation is a small part of a larger commitment to your bigger riding picture. Confidence and a positive sense of self as a performer might start with how you feel, or it might start with a timely positive and affirming statement from someone else. It doesn't matter. Once you approach your ride with polish, your refinement will permeate into other aspects of your ride. Before long, your riding will

In whatever aspect of equestrianism, a well-presented rider gives a distinct impression of precision, self-respect and discipline.

"When you dress for success, you will feel great, your posture will improve, your conviction while riding will improve, and others will reinforce those positive feelings."

Learning how to segment your performance

With a visual picture of how optimal riders present for performance, the next logical theme is how they strategize to achieve peak results. Every type of riding, no matter the discipline, requires well engrained organisation for excellent performance to reveal itself. The correct split second decisions needed for great performance don't just happen. They require deliberate, well-rehearsed strategies with well rehearsed responses. I have always been taught that great mental strategies are built with logic based on chronological progression. Most riding performances have a natural flow to them from beginning to end. Dressage tests, cross-country tests, show jumping tests, and horse races, for instance, follow a clear series of progressive steps, or segments. All of them have a start, all have a segment that can be termed the first few moves, all have a larger main section of performance, all have a winding down segment, and all naturally come to a close. Packaged correctly, rides are meant to unfold into a beautifully designed moving image with horse and rider in symmetry. For them to do so, they need to be planned.

Let's consider the basic dressage test to understand how segmenting works. A first level dressage test has approximately 13-15 desired movements. Considering the test movement by movement is useful when the objective is to ensure that you can complete all the requisite skills separately, each with competence. To perform with optimal success, however, you need to consider the test as an overall performance where movements are seamless, blending from one to the next. From a tactical point of view, the test is meant to be a carryover built out of a positive warm-up, culminating with a discrete start and a clear finish. The test's first segment begins as the dressage rider circles the ring and presents to the judge(s). A rider with a proud posture, a pos-

improve, and soon, it will match with your external image. Consider your daily turnout as you approach your rides, and ask yourself if there is room for image refinement. If you find that there is in fact room for refinement, make the necessary change for at least one week and monitor how it influences how you think, how you feel, how you act, and how you perform as an equestrian. I will wager with you that self-presentation images will enhance your equestrian performance much like it does an elite athlete's. The polished performance image is applicable to every enthusiastic, forward moving equestrian, including you!

Any equestrian performance can be segmented into five or six stages and each stage will have a technical and a tactical aspect.

of physical entry is meant to go unnoticed by horse and rider. Emphasis is placed on a clear, precise, assertive, well balanced, and rhythmic first movement. Afterward, the rider halts, waits a split second, salutes the judge with a smooth and full gesture, gathers the reins, and moves smoothly into the test. As you can see, the start component of the test is as much tactical as it is technical, with both aspects adding to the complete performance picture. From a segmenting perspective, any or all of the strategies outlined within the first part of the dressage test need to be considered with simple one word reminders such as 'straight', 'assert', and 'patience', for instance.

The start is followed in sequence by the first few moves, the main section, the final few movements, and the finishing segment. The first few moves of the dressage test begin with the post-halt ride off, the turning at C, and the following two-three movements. What would a dressage rider's strategy be once the test's movements are in motion? Clearly, one objective is to carry over the momentum from the initial centre line entry. The second objective is to settle both horse and rider into the lovely, accurate rhythm that will follow throughout the entire dressage performance. The test is meant to be harmonious, and the test's harmony is set during the earliest stages of the performance. The main section of the test follows with a well maintained rhythm, close attention to figure and transition accuracy, and impulsion. Every aspect of the performance is meant to be precise, with the horse and rider rhythmically completing each movement to its fullest. Moving forward, the goal with the final few movements is for horse and rider to pay attention to detail, and resist wandering in mind through to the test's completion. Typically, the closing moments of the dressage test are riddled with minor inaccuracies as horses and riders become either tired or impatient. Focus, for the strong performer, doesn't waver from the performance's beginning to end. Mental disci-

itive approach, and the ability to smile and make eye contact with the judge at C leaves a very different impression from the rider who wants to enter quickly, avoid all contact with the judging booth, and complete the class without being noticed too much. Riders are able to establish themselves to different extents, and first images typecast long before the initial salute. Once the rider has portrayed an image of optimism, composure and polish, the bell rings, and it is time to enter the ring. The dressage rider has a sixty second time span, which is an eternity. There is sufficient time to make one last transition when necessary, a few final adjustments, and then smoothly, to line up the center line and entre. The entry is meant to begin well before the rider actually enters the ring, and in fact, the split second

pline of horse and rider are tested during the closing movements, and often, attention perseverance becomes the difference between peak performance and its accompanying elation as compared with mediocrity and regret. The final segment draws the curtain on the performance, and at its optimal, is meant to be like an encore performance. Intensity increases to a higher pitch than onlookers think possible, as judges draw their positive closing reflections while arriving at favourable final impression marks.

As you can see, there are distinct stages to the dressage performance. Similarly, there are distinct segments to every riding performance in terms of routine progression. Your task is to figure out where each of the five-six stages of your performance routine start and finish. In relation to each well defined segment, take the time and develop two aspects, a technical and a tactical component. Within the technical aspect, consider what you have to focus on in terms of aids, transitional accuracy, impulsion, and general technique. As part of the tactical aspect for each segment, list all of the necessary beneficial mental aspects that you need to consider in detail. Examples might include relaxing your shoulders, breathing deeply, staying focused in the moment, and attacking each movement with conviction. Together, the technical and tactical aspects for the test will help you paint and eventually deliver the seamless performance that optimal competition routines are all about. When designing your performance plan by segment, develop an initial draft, and then have your expert coach suggest additional refinements. Afterward, memorize the segment by segment intricacies, practise them during pre-performance training, and take post-ride notes regarding what was included, and what was forgotten. Also, consider whether you would like to refine your plan in any way. As a final suggestion, restrict yourself to no more than four main technical and four main tactical reminders for each segment. If

you have too many aspects to consider within each segment, choose slightly broader terms that encompass your smaller reminders. Start working on your performance plan no less than two weeks before your performance day. It will take you that long to effectively familiarize and integrate all of the necessary aspects that otherwise could compromise your optimal performance.

Simulation training

Enough about written planning for now! As you prepare for your special performance day, much like an actor, you can also benefit from dress rehearsals. Dress rehearsals are practised regularly and effectively by theatre companies before show night arrives. Though equestrians definitely benefit from some aspects of the dress rehearsal formula, I find that athletes and coaches do not use them to their full extent. What comes to your mind when I mention the term dress rehearsal? If you stop and think about it for a moment, there are two aspects to the exercise; 'dress' and 'rehearsal', with both able to play parts in competition preparation. Let's start with rehearsals. As we've already considered, practice is a necessary aspect of the rider's mental readiness. Riders and their coaches need to work together to develop a progressively challenging sequence of routine practice from a typical run-through to more elaborate versions with increased challenges such as steward bit checks, visible judges, and highly populated warm-up arenas. As the rehearsal aspect of practice develops, riders ought to feel a comfortable familiarity with the challenges they are eventually to face in actual performance settings. Through the use of rehearsals, riders and horses are meant to build confidence and familiarity to the point where unknowns are limited, and not limiting. If you were to ask eminent coaches like Jack Legoff, he might reply that good performers are ready for anything!

The second important part of the dress rehearsal is the term 'dress'. I have seen many a show rider wear their riding jackets for the first time in the season as they are readying to enter the ring for their first class. When riding jackets are not practised in before dressage and show jumping tests, they tend to feel tight and restricting. Cross-country riders can suffer equal discomfort from their body protectors as they gallop in an unusually rigid position cross-country. Dressage and hunter riders are meant to practise with their show boots, in part because they often feel slippery and less supple than well-worn training equipment. Along the same lines, horses that are braided need to become accustomed to the tighter than usual feeling of a plaited mane and forelock. Some of the aforementioned equipment, you would probably agree, needs to be practised in generally as the performance season nears. Other aspects including show jackets and plaiting, however, are meant to be integrated at very least during dry run practices the week before the competition. When equipment feels uncomfortable during training, it tends to feel that much less comfortable during the heat of performance. Practise with every part of your riding clothing until it is comfortable. Afterward, you will be ready to perform with comfort when your performance matters most! As a result, your entire focus can be invested in performance and not the limiting distraction of unfamiliarity and accompanied awkwardness.

◎ Practise your performance with every part of your riding clothing until you are comfortable.

Readying before the ride

As you can see, performing has everything to do with systematic planning. The optimal ride is the end product of extensive preparation and commitment on the part of coach and rider. Excellent performance requires talent, but clearly not the misconceived innate talent that encourages or de-motivates many an aspiring rider. The talented rider-horse-coach team that I am referring to is developed systematically through practice and intelligence. The last facet that persistent riders need as part of their preparation formula is a facet that I refer to as 'logistics'. It is one thing to have all the required skills and

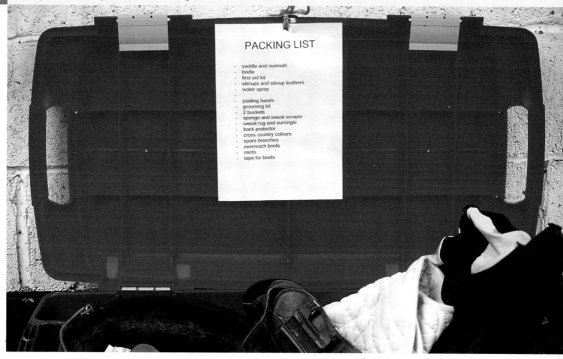

PACKING LIST

- saddle and numnah
- bridle
- first aid kit
- stirrups and stirrup leathers
- water spray

- plaiting bands
- grooming kit
- 2 buckets
- sponge and sweat scraper
- sweat rug and surcingle
- back protector
- cross country colours
- spare breeches
- overreach boots
- mints
- tape for boots

◎ Your packing list will begin with basic requisites but develop as experience indicates the less-obvious necessities.

practice leading up to your performance day, but without an onsite pre-performance plan, readiness is often compromised. The comment I hear from all aspiring performers is: "Great! I have all of the exercises to take me to the competition, but what should I do once I get there?" I have always suggested that the failure to develop an onsite performance plan is clearly a plan destined to fail, and so, I have spent much of my time working with performers as they devise their optimal plans.

When helping equestrians as they develop their logistical onsite plans, I have them stay with the theme of chronological organizing. I have my clients consider their show organization in terms of

- packing;
- departure;
- arrival onsite;
- unloading and greeting;
- show ground familiarization;
- tacking and dressing; and
- warm-ups.

For overnight stays away from home, the additional aspect of night before self-management is also considered. All riders and coaches have actions they could benefit from within each chronological segment leading up to the ideal performance, though few develop a complete structure with a complete list of ingredients for each before segment of performance delivery. The best of performance day organizing leaves riders with the full knowledge that they are systematic, and in full control of themselves, if not the day's progression. Organisation is meant to be somewhat flexible because shows and exhibitions seldom run on correct time, except among the highest level of national and international competitions. And so, there needs to be room among all levels of riders and coaches for some flexibility. However, within the flexible progression leading up to performance, there must also be method to the madness. The key is to remove as many of the nagging questions that end in rider and coach uncertainty as is humanly

Your horse will take his clues regarding optimism and composure from the way in which you handle him from loading to tacking up.

possible. This sub-section devoted to onsite organization will provide you with some ideas regarding how to develop an optimal organization plan for your performance goals.

If I were to tell you that even the most experienced of performers forget some article of equipment when they pack, would you believe me? When

I worked as a member of the Canadian Olympic Committee's administrative staff at two international major games early in my professional development, I was astounded to learn that at least one athlete or coach from almost every national team, even during the most important of competitions, suffer from packing oversights. The end result is always the same. The suffering athlete panics, and afterwards, tries to recover self-composure while looking to borrow an unfamiliar piece of equipment from another hopefully generous competitor or teammate. Small oversights of forgetfulness leave rider and coach with a self-perception of sloppiness, and an image among others of disorganization. As we discussed earlier, impression management and confidence are built from considering yourself, and also, from the information you gain from others in the performance environment. With a weakened image comes diminished confidence and less conviction, all the while with the performance drawing nearer. Therefore, I always suggest a packing list. Look through most performance related riding books, and you can find at least one example of a packing list. Typically, packing lists emphasize horse and rider performance equipment. When you develop your list, I also recommend that you include casual clothing, music, bottles of water, and if appropriate, meal supplements. Obviously, the elite level competitor's list will require more detail to reconcile the length of trip, and potentially, an overseas aspect. Regardless, though, a well suited list is important, and a copy of it should be placed on the inside of every trunk that you travel with. When packing, use a master list and check off each ingredient as it is placed in its appropriate container. That way, you will be removing some of the concerns that haunt the typical performer as he or she travels to the competition site. Performers should never travel to their show settings, all the while wondering whether they have forgotten something. What a waste of energy that would be!

The next two stages of logistical planning are departure and arrival. Departure includes the loading of equipment and the loading of horses. Both need to be loaded in a systematic and caring way, because ultimately, your diligence will ensure that both arrive in sound condition. Horse loading is of particular importance, with the horse taking its cues regarding optimism and composure from you. If you are rushed and impatient, your horse might become defensive, and if not, it will worry about the journey and what is to come afterward. Horses are meant to enjoy their trailer experiences, and you are meant to reflect the very same composed person you typically are, even as the challenge of competition/exhibition approaches. With a consistent approach from day to day training onward to competition, your horse will learn the very same consistent worry-free formula, a formula which happens to be essential for long-term performance success. Afterward, travel is supposed to be enjoyable. The physical journey toward your performance moment is meant to be fun, and your approach needs to reflect that philosophy. Performance opportunities are exactly that, opportunities! Many competitors of all ages forget that their equestrian pursuits began as an enjoyable activity. While travelling, listen to music, enjoy the company of those who are journeying with you, and closely monitor your horse throughout.

The next step in the journey to performance is marked by the arrival at the show ground. How you choose to self-manage while off loading, and while approaching officials and stewards, sets a tone for the build up and delivery of your approaching performance. The rider who is unsettled, disorganized and impatient shows clear signs of uncertainty, self-questioning, and pessimism. In contrast, the rider who is settled, composed, enthusiastic, receptive and clear-minded displays performance enhancing behaviours. To perform at your best, you need to be relaxed, happy, approachable, and yet, focused on

◎ The rider who is composed, enthusiastic and approachable is the rider who will perform at his or her best.

you! For some people, the most important part of performance is the social aspect that goes along with it. For the aspiring performer, socializing and rapport building is secondary, even though an image of good conduct and fair play are crucial to long-term persistence and meaning. I suggest that you enjoy your arrival at the venue, and meet and greet others with kindness and enthusiasm. However, remember that the main players in your performance package are those who prepared along with you: your horse and your coach. It is these latter two, and you, who must be at centre stage leading up to show time.

With the excitement of arrival and unpacking completed, a scouting of the exhibition grounds is time well spent. Each time I travel to an international competition with athletes and coaches, together we dedicate at least one hour in order to study the intricacies of the grounds. We look for access to water, food, vet care, blacksmiths, scoreboards, washrooms, and finally, the warm-up and performance rings. Information about each of these aspects tends to become an important part of your performance day functioning. I suggest leaving the warm-up and performance ring scouting for last, in part because doing so helps the performer narrow in focus to the central agenda: showing. When considering the warm-up ring, it is worth considering its size, its footing, what it might look like filled with competitors, and where tack stewards will be situated. Though all of these concerns are logistical, they are important and need to be answered before warm-up time. The competition ring must be looked at last as performers narrow their focus even further to the ride, itself. Consider the physical layout of the ring, what riding in it might feel like, and where judges and the audience will be seated. Finally, find a quiet place, and undisturbed, return to the imagery you learned during Chapter Five. Complete a positive and detailed mental run through of your upcoming performance using your postural technique. After doing so, relax, and acknowledge that you are mentally ready to perform, and remember the detailed progression you followed in order to feel the certainty that you now feel.

The final pre-ride stage includes three parts: grooming, tacking and dressing. If you are preparing your own mount for performance, start with you! Allow yourself enough time to dress slowly

and methodically. Pull your pressed shirt off the hanger and notice its crispness and its beautifully formed creases. Follow the very same process when putting on your riding pants. Afterward, put your freshly polished boots on, and if appropriate, do up your tie. Take one second and look in the mirror. How do you look? Do you appear polished? Check your posture. Are you carrying yourself as a successful high level performer would? It is show time, and you have to look and feel the part! Once you are ready, it is time to provide the horse with the very same courtesy. Spend as much time on your horse as you did on yourself, all the while making much of its appearance. Horses need to feel proud, too! Both of you must appear beautifully turned out, because together, you are shortly meant to meld into a well prepared and aesthetically pleasing image. Once you have groomed your horse, tack it up, and afterward, give the tack one last dusting, take a step back and look at the picture in front of you. What you should see is a well turned out and sparkling mount, who is keenly appraising you in much the same way! You are ready to mount and reveal the detailed preparation that you followed leading up to your special moment. Again, don't forget what you did to get to where you are now. Good performances require detailed preparation, and you need to know that you have done your job completely.

It is with the knowledge that you are ready, that you are meant to approach your warm-up. Warm-ups at their best follow the very same methodical structure that typical schooling rides do. They are supposed to start slowly, with you horse recognizing that you are the very same composed person who typically enjoys its efforts and abilities. Your focus is meant to narrow even further when compared with earlier onsite stages of preparing.

You can develop an awareness of those around you, who are also in the midst of readying for performance. However, your primary focus must tar-

 Time spent in the warm up arena is used to prepare horse and rider for the forthcoming performance.

get your horse-rider combination, in some instances with some external guidance from your coach. Slowly, the warm-up aspect of your ride is meant to progress in momentum as you both warm through the most relevant of movements or demands, be they flat or jumping. All the while, you are best served by a quiet, certain, and positive perspective, a perspective that is meant to reassure both performers - horse and rider. As I said earlier, at its ideal, the warm-up is meant to be

gradual, with its progression logically and seamlessly taking both athletes to the performance arena. The warm-up, in summary, is meant to prepare both horse and rider for a performance that James Wofford, former United States Equestrian Team rider, likens to a crucible. The horse and rider's sole intention, through the warm-up stage, is to ensure that the pair's full abilities reveal themselves, with no residual unkept aspects of the performance left untouched.

Flow: The end product

When the time to perform arrives, there are three general types of experience that horse and rider can go through. For the rider who hasn't prepared methodically, the ride, at best, might require step by step strategic thinking, with the rider focused in the moment on what to do next. Through a logical in-the-moment approach, the ride will feel and appear mechanically sound and accurate. All of the necessary components of the performance will be visible, as the rider makes both technical and tactical decisions. The second possibility for the performer coming from incomplete preparation is elevated and undermining performance anxiety. The anxious performer tends to focus on the managing of personal nerves, at least in part, while also attempting to put forward a reasonable performance. With energy diffused through two demands as opposed to one, self-control and performance exhibition, the ride becomes deliberate, unsteady, and tentative. Though the first of these two options is clearly the best response to incomplete readiness, the sort of preparation we've been building toward in this chapter leads to an entirely different and more rewarding third option: flow.

When equestrians are fully prepared for the riding challenges they are facing, they experience feelings of certainty and privilege. Riders at their best moments are meant to approach their performances with a distinct belief that every possible performance concern has been uncovered and addressed through daily training and pre-performance preparation. With a complete confidence founded on hard work, dedication and systematic preparation, the horse and rider can prepare to "let go" and deliver the skills that have been integrated within them. Have you ever experienced a moment in time where you were completely absorbed in a task? While you were engaged, I will bet that you lost track of time, and that your body, your mind, and the task became

one. If you have not experienced complete engagement within a ride, consider a time where you experienced complete focus either in your job, during studies, or even while you were reading a book or chatting with friends. No doubt you have experienced complete focus at one time or another in your life.

For the equestrian who is completely prepared, engagement is likely to surface on its own during performance opportunities. During the fully engaged ride, horse and rider become one, and deliberate thought is replaced by intuitive decision making and automatic response. I can recall the performance of one memorable dressage ride at a national competition, where my horse and I scored eighty-eight percent, an unusually high score, and we amassed nine 10's from a single judge. The test ought to have been memorable, but to be honest I can't remember its particulars as well as the overall experience. What I can recall is that the performance was complete, and that its delivery seemed to spring out of my horse and I without much physical and mental effort. In addition, it seemed as if we both enjoyed the experience, with the test's demands seen as secondary to the primary ambition of harmony.

Some might indicate that only the most experienced of riders are capable of achieving optimal peak performance. Those sorts of self-handicapping responses are false, and only serve to limit the aspiring equestrian's short-term hopes. Every rider at every level is capable of experiencing flow performance, including you! Extensive training and a complete preparation package will take you several very large steps forward toward flow experience. However, there is still one more aspect that you will need to take you the rest of the way. As part of my last book, Focused Riding, I devoted an entire chapter to a theme I termed 'the leap of faith'. Knowing that you are ready and able to deliver excellence is a necessary part of great performances, but it is incomplete on its own. You also need to believe through to your very core that your horse and rider combination will deliver a complete package when faced with performance challenges. Through belief, you must be willing to let go of your inhibitions, and place trust in the time and energy you previously devoted to readying. It is through the final skills of trusting and letting go that flow rides finally surface. There are few riders willing to place complete trust in their preparation, even when that preparation is complete. You need to be the exception to the norm, not the rule. Letting go requires practice, and as an end result, there are few experiences more rewarding. Trust your preparation, trust your coach, trust your horse, trust yourself, and let go! Take the risk, and leave no regrets in your wake!

The post-performance evaluation and integration

All performances come to an end, and each ending brings new beginnings. The stellar equestrian embraces past performance experiences, learns what needs to be learned from each one, integrates its lesson, and moves forward. Post-performance evaluations are a rewarding and necessary step that completes every preparation and performance cycle. With a clear evaluation of what works, and what requires additional refinement, the coach and rider gain additional knowledge and additional tools to be integrated in future preparation and performance cycles. With knowledge comes the possibility of further development, and an accompanied feeling of optimism. It is crucial that every rider considers where to go from here, how to get there, what to do, and what to avoid. I have been witness to equestrians who overlook the post-performance evaluation stage entirely, and with it, forego the

much needed insights that lead to sustained progression. Instead, some riders choose to assign successes to their own abilities, and their setbacks to their horses or the people around them. Learning requires a level of truthfulness and diligence that only some equestrians are willing to entertain. Consider your personal role in each performance, both good and bad, as well as the role of your horse, the role of your coach, and the role of additional mitigating circumstances. In collaboration with your coach, work on the emerging lessons, and afterward, the refining steps that will take you forward to your equestrian goals.

If you look through the book shelves of your local book store or library, you will find several different debriefing methods suggested by sport psychology and coaching authors. To be honest, there is no wrong way of evaluating your performance after the fact. I do, however, suggest a few key rules for you to consider. One suggestion relates to timeframe. Evaluations should be done at two separate times. The first part should be completed within the 24 hour timeframe immediately after the performance while its technical intricacies are fresh in your mind. Technical lessons are vivid, and there are often many of them to document. Were there specific things that you did during the performance that added or took away from the outcome? For instance, were your aids perfect or overly strong during one specific transition or during the approach to a specific obstacle? Take a sheet of lined paper, and develop two columns, with one column assigned to optimal aspects, and one column devoted to aspects that were weak. Be thorough and try to recall as many details as you can. If you have available video footage, a visual review will also jog your memory. The second part of the evaluation should be completed within 48 hours of performance completion. Within this second part, consider more general technical and tactical progressions of the competition/exhibition in relation to each aspect

Post-competition evaluations are a necessary step in the performance cycle.

of your preparation and onsite management. Were you well prepared? Were your simulations appropriate and with sufficient detail? Review every chronological segment in detail, identify which aspects you intend to maintain during future performances, and which you intend to modify.

After you have completed the written post-performance review, make an appointment at the earliest possible time to review your insights with your coach. As part of the meeting, share what you have learned from the recent performance, and what you hope to carry over to future performances. Once you have shared your insights, your coach will certainly provide you with additional insights that you might have overlooked. During this process, take notes. As the saying goes 'two heads are better than one'. Your coach will agree with at least part of your review, and the review will provide an opportunity for shared understanding. In addition, your coach will provide you with additional suggestions founded on professional experience and credibility. With the advantage of your firsthand experience, and your coach's suggestions, meld both into a refined plan that you can implement during your next performance. With each preparation-performance-evaluation cycle, your competition/exhibition package will slowly take shape, with the riding objective you have always wanted as its end. As a final note, take some time and acknowledge the fun that you are experiencing as you pursue equestrian excellence. Riding is meant to be an enjoyable and rewarding experience. The pleasure you will gain from meeting your goals and learning new skills will sustain long after specific memories and your pursuit of riding development has passed.

Getting started

The topic of competition planning is an important aspect of riding performance. Its application can be widespread, meaning that you can use preparation and performance tactics in everything you do, especially during all aspects of equestrianism. Every rider needs to be up for the challenge being pursued, and every rider needs to learn how to integrate the mental and physical skills they have already learned in the heat of performance. Competitors can clearly integrate every chronological aspects of the performance package we have considered in this chapter. But wait a minute, so too can pleasure riders hoping to meet new challenges, foxhunters attempting their first hunt in jumping country, and both

types of racing jockeys. After all, performance preparation is beneficial in any situation where people are readying to face a challenge. There are specific things that you can do leading up to a challenge, and during that challenge, that will bring out the best in you! All that is needed is a little diligence on your part. The insights you will gain from an exploration of what brings out the best in you and your horse will take you forward into territory where some equestrians opt not to venture. I suggest that you explore your uncharted performance territory and learn what it has to offer you. I promise that your exploration will be interesting, if not profound.

General Tips
- Performance is a day in and day out process. It is practised during daily training, and then transported to the performance arena.
- Horse and rider immaculate turnout is a daily endeavor that will enhance your rides. Ensure that you are properly turned out each day and that you exude confidence through your posture.
- Simulate progressive challenges during your daily training before performing.
- Flow performances are the end product of good preparation and the willingness to let go.
- Take the time to debrief after each performance. Performances can provide you with useful information that you can integrate during future performances.

8. Perspective and performance in equestrianism

With the closing stages of this book in sight, it is important that we take a step back and consider equestrian performance from a broader perspective. Perspective is often an unspoken theme in equestrianism, even though it is the fabric that holds every equestrian's sport pursuits intact. In equestrianism, there are two willing partners, both seeking to reach an understanding with the other. During their modest beginnings, horse and rider approach riding as a special sport, one with a lot to offer, and so they should! There is no other sport that offers such benefits. Equestrianism offers the opportunity for horse and rider to share communication in a way that transcends species. It is the only sport where two very different physical entities can meld as one while dancing together, while galloping through nature, while jumping all sizes and types of obstacles, and even while, together, pursuing Olympic dreams! Somehow, horse and rider have managed to reach an understanding where the rider is welcomed onto the horse's back, with both partners accepting different roles in the pursuit of ambitious shared experiences. Riding is definitely a sport out of the ordinary!

The challenge of maintaining a healthy and positive perspective for the equestrian, however, is sometimes trying. Equestrian training facilities and show grounds are riddled with a wide variety of horse-rider

combinations. The term "horseman" is the highest of compliments paid to any horse enthusiast, in part because it is a label meant to exemplify a group of riders and coaches with the clearest of perspectives. Horse people, according to what I have learned, are those who are methodical and kind to mounts. Horse people are able to understand the challenges of training, hear the concerns of their horses, and respond with sympathy and reassurance. With the ability to understand and sympathize, horse people build trust with their equine partners, and slowly, both willingly move forward and evolve as one in a process of shared learning. With understanding also comes perspective. Learning happens naturally, when it is ready to happen, and not before. After all, both members of the equine partnership are part of a team in search of partnership first, and performance second. Teams that exhibit good horsemanship learn together, struggle together, and yes, they also play together. Harmonious teams with a positive perspective can be found at all levels of equestrian performance, and in all of the equestrian disciplines.

There is also a second group of coaches, riders and horses to be found at training sites and competition venues. This second group employs an entirely different perspective of equestrianism that is geared entirely toward performance. Look carefully at almost

⊚ The original pleasure that you found in your favourite sport must not be sacrificed to the need to achieve peak performance, resulting in anger and hostility.

every riding venue and you will find riders who bare an unhappy expression upon completion of a lesson or exhibition despite having had yet another opportunity to experience their favourite sport: riding. The ride and its merits seem lost during those unfortunate moments. You can also search out riders engaged in arguments with their personal support system, all the while exposing their uneasy horses to escalating levels of anger and hostility. As a third possibility, there are equestrians who discipline their mounts for mistakes that are often-times unintentionally committed and the result of mutual misunderstanding. This last concern is the most serious of all, given that the horse is no longer a willing partner in the pursuit of riding goals. Instead, conformity, harmony, and willingness are replaced with an approach intended to inspire obedience without agreement. There is an underlying sadness embedded in all of these examples of lost perspective. The joy of riding is sometimes misplaced by equestrians, even among those who are typically the most caring of people.

This chapter will address the more positive aspects of perspective. It is easy to explain what is wrong with impatience, intolerance, lack of understanding, and lost values in the sport of equestrian. However, as you know, more productive thoughts and emotions are gained by considering a positive example, than a negative one. Within riding, positive thoughts and positive examples inspire good decisions, good experiences, more enthusiasm, and so, the ongoing pursuit of "good" equestrian dreams. Equestrianism is a privilege that we must acknowledge, savour, appreciate, instill and support in those around us. A positive model of horsemanship and perspective is something that you and I are consistently capable of even though the positive is sometimes lost for a moment. Every rider and coach is capable of learning and relearning positive perspective. Some might counter that with: "As equestrians, we have to be realists. It is not always possible to maintain a positive perspective, and it is not always possible to remain patient." In response, know this: people have been gifted with the ability to reason. You can choose to adopt a positive approach to each ride, and you can choose to appreciate each equestrian experience for what it has to offer. You have been gifted with free choice, and with it comes tremendous responsibili-ty. In equestrianism, that responsibility is not only to yourself and those around you, but also to your collaborative partner, the horse.

A Personal Anecdote

A few years ago, upon completion of my doctorate, I began competing in dressage. I enjoyed the sport immensely. During one memorable competition, I was entered in my first FEI level classes against a number of successful developing international calibre horse and rider combinations. My wife and I departed to the competition very early in the morning the day before the competition began, as we had a six hour drive to the venue, and we were concerned about how our horse would manage travelling in the heat. The expected temperature that day was 90 degrees Fahrenheit, and the humidity was forecasted as high. We arrived at the venue mid-morning, picked up our bridle number, offloaded our horse, watered and bathed him, set up his stall, settled him in, and slowly went about unpacking as he relaxed. Our job was completed by noon, and so we explored the show grounds. As we reached the training and competition areas, we noticed that there were many serious competitors training their horses during the heat of the day. The riders and their horses were hot and irritated. When we watched the riders' facial expressions, no enjoyment was evident. Instead, we were under the distinct impression that the riders we were witnessing viewed their tune-up rides as an activity to be completed on a set time schedule, much like an executive schedules office meetings.

Our philosophy was somewhat different. We were not going to exercise and tune-up our horse in the heat of the day. The exertion would be unnecessary given that large portions of energy were required for the following day's performance. Instead, we sat down to a light lunch under the shade of a large oak tree, watched the others school for a few minutes, and then journeyed to the farthest and quietest point of the show grounds. There, we found another large oak tree that offered shade and relief from the day's unforgiving heat. My wife spread out a large blanket, and we stretched out with our two dogs for an afternoon nap. Two hours later, we woke up, rested, rejuvenated, happy, and ready to train. By the time we tacked our horse, it was late afternoon, and the heat was manageable. Our training that night was enjoyable and undemanding. The following morning, I was scheduled to ride at 09:00. As the warm-up progressed, I found that my horse was in a particularly good mood. I made the tactical decision that day to let go, and the ride became an amazing experience. Though we were newcomers to the FEI dressage levels, we were placed second in a class of forty well regarded national and international competitors. I will confess that there were far more experienced dressage combinations within our class than my horse and I. Fortunately for us, though, few riders that weekend adopted the same relaxed and enjoyment filled approach that my wife, my horse and I did. It was through our healthy perspective that I recognized the important marriage of fun and success when facing adversity.

Explaining perspective

Many people wonder what perspective is, and how perspective is learned. It seems that riders stumble onto perspective reminders during unanticipated opportune moments. Equestrians experience moments of perspective when they are riding at sunrise, when they are galloping with a sense of freedom in nature, and even when they are playing with their horses in a muddy or dusty paddock. Perspective happens when we stop for a moment and realize that: "Hey, I am having fun right now doing something that I typically forget to appreciate. This experience feels rewarding and rejuvenating. Wow!" During those special moments, our enjoyment is unanticipated, and it is surprising. Yet, when we think about each special moment afterwards, it makes perfect sense. Perspective happens when we relax, when we slow ourselves down, and we consider how we fit with nature, its serenity, and its creatures. On the other hand, when we move at a quick pace, live on the razor's edge, focus entirely on ourselves, and forget those around us, we remain out of touch with the world. In essence, we let go of our grasp on perspective.

Every now and again, even the busiest of people is reminded that perspective is important. People with serious health issues often realize the importance of perspective, only once they are compelled to slow down, self-reflect and consider where they fit in relation to those around them.

Equestrianism can be a blessing when it comes to the learning and relearning of perspective. Horses are patient teachers; they humble us, and sometimes when we listen carefully, they try to engage us in play. Horses are not rushed without consequence. Rewards in riding sometimes take time, and for them to happen, horses insist that we share with them in fun and in pranks, as well as in work. Horses are not clockwork operations, and they do not understand the relevance of today's fast moving pace, our busy sched-

Like Blyth Tait and Ready Teddy, some riders develop such an understanding and communication with their horses that their names become forever linked.

ules, internet access, and the global economy. In contrast, what they do understand is that performance is built on perspective and rapport. Only riders with perspective and a broadened approach to riding fully benefit from what their horses have to offer. Horses insist it is so, and there is little their riders can do about it other than to conform when the goal is optimal performance! An understanding of perspective in equestrianism is a big part of being a stellar student of our sport. Therefore, it is time that we each build on the perspective we have as we approach our equestrian pursuits.

When we consider our horse-rider combination's development as a balanced approach with some training, some low intensity relaxation, and some high intensity fun, progress ensues. When balance is compromised at the expense of overtraining, horse and rider lose their enthusiasm, and what was initially fun becomes a pressure filled or boring task. Riding is meant to be a release for both horse and rider. That is how young horses and novice riders initially approach their shared partnership, with a beginner's mind. Yet, many riders evolve into aspiring equestrians who are entirely task driven. The misguided loss of fun and spontaneity is a grave error. Perspective, and with it, the beginner's mindset, need to be guarded with diligence each day. The consequence of not doing so at best is a loss in meaning and a loss of passion suffered at the hands of a potentially meaningful sport. At worst, there are many riders and coaches lost to new sports, and many horses lost to irreversible apathy and distrust.

Recalling the initial riding approach

The term 'beginner's mind' is not new among sport psychology enthusiasts. It was mentioned by John Lynch, an eminent sport and life con-

sultant from California more than ten years ago. When I initially stumbled upon the term, I did not understand exactly what was meant by a 'beginner's mind'. I thought that the term sounded esoteric, and lacking in substance. Today, I understand the importance of all terms holding the potency to stimulate large portions of optimism and receptiveness within each of us. When are people most optimistic and receptive, you probably wonder? The answer is simple: at the beginning of a learning curve. Try to recall your first experiences as an equestrian in order to understand what I mean. I will wager that you looked forward to your weekly lessons, as I did! You probably spent countless time with your horse in its stall grooming, and even feeding it carrots and apples. Every time you mounted, your heart probably missed a beat, and your breathing rate increased a little. You were excited to ride! You probably woke up the morning of each riding session early, with a spring in

◎ Recapturing the enthusiasm and optimism that accompanied early riding experiences is your most important sport psychology task.

◎ Collect together some of your equestrian keepsakes and explore the emotions that accompany the memories they bring.

your step. You probably couldn't wait to get out to the stables. Riding was special, you saw it as special, and you approached it with a level of enthusiasm that was invigorating.

When I interviewed a large group of Olympic athletes [including equestrians] some years ago as part of a scientific research project, each had the opportunity to speak about his and her career evolution as a world renowned athlete. When I asked the athletes about experiences travelling with their national teams, all mentioned without exception that their first season at the international level was the most enjoyable. Each athlete spoke with glowing eyes about that first special season, that first special coaching staff, and the first group of exceptionally co-operative teammates. Everything within the first year of performing at the international

al level was positive and memorable. As each athlete elaborated on the years that followed, a lot of the experiences shared sounded mundane, boring, and task like. The athletes sounded like they were employees, not athletes in the pursuit of excellence. In essence, they had lost their beginner's mentality.

Riders of all levels go through this very same process if they are not careful in noticing each day's special experiences. With the arrival of familiarity, contempt seems to follow. Riding proficiency is important in order for the equestrian to move forward and develop. However, proficiency without a beginner's mind erodes at enthusiasm, perspective, and balance. Maintaining a beginner's mind is, perhaps, your most important sport psychology task. Start looking through your horse memorabilia. If you have old pictures from the beginning of your riding adventures, pull them out, and place them in a smaller album. Look for the initial riding books that you acquired. If you are anything like me, you probably have a general book about grooming and horsemanship! Also, dig out your first items of riding equipment and take a good look at it. Do you have any initial mementos from your first horseshow, or exhibition? Do you have any small keepsakes from your first set of lessons or your first school horse? Perhaps you can find your first crop, your first bridle, or your first pair of spurs. I recall that at the beginning, I used to collect horseshoes like they were the most prized of possessions the world had to offer. I still have one horseshoe from my early past.

Once you have amassed a series of keepsakes that seem to spark your memories a little, explore each memory separately. What sorts of emotions seem to be surfacing? What can you recall as your initial approach to riding? How did you feel about your first coach? Can you remember the first horse you ever rode? My first horse's name was "Chum".

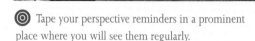

Tape your perspective reminders in a prominent place where you will see them regularly.

As you start reliving past memories, notice how you are feeling about your riding. While you have some vivid memories at the forefront, pull out your performance journal and write down the single statements that together encompass your beginner's mind as a novice equestrian. If you are a coach, do the very same task from a novice coach's perspective as opposed to a novice rider's. Once you have completed your task, turn to the next page and compare your initial riding approach with the one you are currently engaged in. Be thorough, and also, be entirely honest with yourself. Are there any differences? The evaluation of your current riding perspective complete, grab a coloured marker and underline at least two aspects within your current approach that would benefit from a little more enthusiasm. Write both perspective reminders down on two 3.5 x 5.0 inch index cards. Tape one index card to the inside of your equipment box, and the second card beside your bridle hook. Before each ride, review your perspective reminders and take a few minutes to consider how you will integrate each reminder during your upcoming ride. Then, with a strong perspective in place, enjoy your ride, and notice how your horse responds. I promise you that there is a lot to be said for practising the beginner's mindset each day!

Considering the bigger picture

Equestrianism is an amazing sport! As I mentioned before, it teaches each of us ample lessons about horses, about ourselves, and about life in general. The successful equestrian definitely must be willing to hear lessons from each of these three sources in order to progress as a complete horse person. As riders, first, we are compelled to hear the voice of our mounts. Though horses clearly cannot speak, they are expressive in interesting ways. A horse that is glad to see you, listens for your voice, and upon first sign, moves to the front of its stall with excited anticipation. Horses are expressive when they are pulled out of their stalls, when they are groomed, when they are tacked, when they are mounted, when they are ridden, when they are dismounted, and when they are returned to their stalls. The 'tuned in' equestrian notices the unspoken signals of their mount, acknowledges each one, allays fears, and encourages hope and optimism. By understanding the horse, the rider is rewarded with an harmonious partnership, and many special moments at unexpected times. Through the ability to hear our horses, we also invite them to hear us. There are instances when each one of us needs to be heard, and horse and rider can provide one another with wisdom and perspective during those special teachable moments.

As riders, we also are provided with the ongoing possibility of self-reflection and life lessons. With each equine challenge that arises, we respond. There are instances when every equestrian responds with impatience, perhaps out of fear and perhaps out of intolerance and aggravation. There are also more positive moments when, as riders, we respond to the uncertainty of our mounts with tolerance and compassion. Each horse behaviour and each riding circumstance can evoke a number of different responses in every one of us. Some of our responses will be good responses, and others will undermine our self-confidence, and perhaps our self-concept. Good and bad, all of our responses can teach us something about ourselves. You, for instance, might realize that you are a lot more patient than even you believed after experiencing uncertainty or scary circumstances such as a bolting horse. I learned early on that I was intolerant of personal rider and horse mistakes, and that I had to become more forgiving of both of us. Like some of my colleagues, I also tended to overemphasize structured learning over fun and relaxing rides. These sorts of imbalances provide ample suggestion regarding possibilities for positive change. Your tendencies as a horseperson will provide you with a wide number of opportune moments to learn all about your strengths and weaknesses as a rider, and as a performer on the stage of life. With each lesson will come the opportunity to deliberately maintain the best of your responses, and to deliberately refine the weaker ones. Beforehand, though, notice after each important tactical decision that you make whether your emotional response is happiness and pride, guilt, or shame. Each response that you choose as a rider and as an equestrian will evoke a personal reaction, and only some will be immediately welcoming. Embrace every lesson that you learn, and its reward will echo into every aspect of your development.

The time to train

I mentioned earlier that there is a time for each horse-rider partnership to play, a time to relax, and yes, there obviously is a time to train. Training is an important aspect of the horse and rider's shared learning. Though playing and relaxing have a lot to offer the equestrian partnership, and I will get to the importance of each soon, your equine partnership ought also to benefit from mental stimulation and challenge. Generally speaking, how do you feel about learning something new? Personally, I seek out new learning opportunities in my chosen profession and hobbies every chance I get! You undoubtedly do the same. I can say so with confidence given the fact that you bought this book, which happens to be geared toward equestrian learning. Within each schooling or competitive opportunity that you are exposed to, there clearly are lessons to be gained. There are lessons learned about you and your horse from great performances, good performances, moderate performances, and weak performances. Without a search, and afterward, an understanding of what you need to focus on in order to move forward, there is little reason for you to assume room for growth. Without the possibility of personal growth, motivation and confidence eventually waver. Why would anyone look forward to their daily equestrian activities when they found themselves at a prolonged standstill? We all need eternal signs of hope, and only with the promise of refinement can we sustain our optimism as equestrians over time.

Though every equestrian holds the opportunity to learn new skills, and hone old ones, those opting for a healthy perspective ought to consider each riding experience, good and bad, in relation to a more general backdrop of performance. Riding lessons and refinements are meant to be gifts that take the equestrian forward to proficiency in one aspect of life. Every rider's life is comprised of many different aspects including sport, education, a professional career, and personal relationships, for instance. Together, these aspects are meant to provide a broadened perspective that adds clarity and dimension for each one of us. There is nothing earth shattering about a poor day's ride. Similarly, great rides are not meant to eclipse professional activities, personal relationships, nor financial responsibilities. The steps forward and the setbacks experienced within equestrianism are meant to be regarded as part of a grander scheme, not as the grander scheme. It makes no difference whether you are a recreational equestrian or an aspiring Olympian, maintain a broad perspective and consider your day to day riding experiences as part of life's grander scheme.

◎ Great rides should be seen as part of the grander scheme and not the grander scheme itself.

Seize each opportunity to have fun in your riding activities.

A time for play

In my past life, I was a coach of competition riders. I coached novice junior competitors, Continental Young Riders from several different geographical regions, adult recreational hopefuls, and even a few senior national team aspirants. During the process, I learned that training was important, and that it worked best when balanced with play times. Much like young children, we all need a time to play and interact without pressure. Riding can provide exactly that opportunity when allowed to.

The riders I worked with sometimes ended off group lessons with games, including red light - green light. The key within the "light game" was to have riders and their horses practise general control in a safe and fun environment. The last rider to stop when I called "red light" was returned to the starting line at the back of the group. Those first to move forward after the calling of "green light" were promoted with additional steps closer to the finish line. The intention was to have horses and riders with sharpened skills, and moreover, the intention was to place both parts of every equestrian team in a situation where they had to rely on each other while in a fun circumstance. Learning and rapport seem to go hand in hand, and both can sometimes be bolstered without direct intention.

Far too often, riders and coaches overlook the importance of having fun for the horse, rider, and coach triad. More time needs to be allocated by equestrians in the pursuit of fun. Even in circumstances that do not end with lessons, something is learned. The best of horse and rider relationships are forged in opportune and unusual moments and unusual circumstances. When horse, rider, and coach arrive at the point where they can have fun together and enjoy each other's company as an end in itself, only then have they truly arrived at the destination of complete rapport. With a rapport built on solid training and fun memories, the equestrian team of horse, rider, and coach meld into a polished entity able to respond with confidence to every challenge. Remember that the journey in riding is as important as the destination. Part of that journey must be founded on experiences and memories of sheer enjoyment. At first, you might have to schedule fun activities into your riding activities deliberately.

However, with time, fun opportunities will reveal themselves more easily, and with practice, you will be ready to seize each one. Remember that your long-term optimistic perspective is built on a freshness that typically is only experienced by new comers to our sport, people approaching their rides with the aim of having fun! Activities that instil fun in your equestrian pursuits will lead you to the sustained pursuit of riding excellence.

A time to slow down

As an equestrian, there are also times when slowing down becomes the order of the day. When you consider what slowing down implies there are a number of different meanings. Slowing down could refer to the winding down segment at the beginning and end of each ride, it could refer to rides with little or no intensity, and it could refer to a general plan of horse and rider progression. Returning to a low intensity at the beginning and end of each ride ties in with perspective because well attended horses are warmed and cooled slowly at the end of each training session. The intention with low intensity is a building of positive perspective from one ride's beginning, to its ending, to the beginning of the next ride in an ongoing cycle of increasing optimism. Within each ride, then, there is meant to be room allotted for "warming in" and "cooling out". Both aspects of each ride are meant to provide the horse and rider with time for reflection and rapport. When this cyclical process is overlooked, on the other hand, both horse and rider suffer from a loss of perspective. Every aspect of each ride is a commitment of time and complete focus to one task, the horse and rider partnership. When clocks are watched, and steps within each ride are compromised, the initial intention of equestrian development suffers. Once rides are completed in their entirety, right down to the final grooming, and the returning of tack to its hook or box, only then is the rider free to push onward to another task. Riding experiences are yours to enjoy, and

they are meant to be relished in the moment from beginning to end. Be mindful of where you are in each moment in relation to where you need to be.

Slowing down can also refer to the general pace you choose within a ride. There are times when a low intensity ride in solitude becomes a good opportunity to listen to yourself and your horse. Riding in solitude can be rejuvenating when rider and horse engage in a long and low session in the privacy of an indoor arena, and even more so when they ride in nature. Where I ride out of doors, there is a beautiful dirt road with a fast running creek, surrounded by gorgeous hills complete with wildlife. There are days when training becomes too intense, or my professional responsibilities become pressure filled. Recognizing that either my horse or I are overwhelmed, I have been known to opt for the refuge of nature. After one full hour of relaxation with only the company of our partnership, we have both returned to the stables with a quieter mindset. There are times when every horse and rider combination yearns for a low intensity ride. After all, no living entity can sustain daily pressure without the consequence of burnout and compromised health. By intentionally slowing down your ride, you can plan for the ebbs and flows of riding development and life. Further, tranquil opportunities will provide you with less external distractions, and more time to build a rapport without the pressure of immediate performance productivity. Balance and perspective first, and productivity along with performance follow.

Perhaps the most important possible meaning for 'slowing down' refers to the bigger picture of horse and rider long-term development. Within every corner of our global equestrian community, there are partnerships that progress at the wrong pace in the pursuit of their objectives. I have been witness to horses and riders that have been moved along in their progress too quickly and too slowly. Both of these planning errors are equally dam-

⊚ Riding in solitude can be a rejuvenating experience when training becomes too intense or profession responsibilities overwhelming.

aging to the equestrian partnership, but for different reasons. The horse and rider placed on too steep a learning curve often experience rapid short-term improvements, and afterward, the long-term discovery of personal limitations in riding skills and in self-confidence. With a premature discovery of limitations, horse and rider struggle to surpass earlier foundational setbacks as they attempt to regain a beginner's mindset, and the uninhibited efforts of earlier days. Under-faced riders suffer from the very same lack of confidence and positive experiences as those who are over-faced. There are some coaches who handicap the

progression of their riders, and there are more riders who self-handicap their learning due to a fear of failure. Those who are slow to progress never fail, but sadly, they never gain the satchel of positive experiences that end in increased self-confidence and the realization of dreams. For both groups, perspective is lost to fear and inhibition, often when all that stands in the way is exposure to the unfamiliar. With a broadened perspective comes the realization that, often-times, our inhibitions are only depriving us of an even better quality of life with more fun and more optimism than previously experienced.

Getting started

You obviously agree with me that equestrianism is an amazing sport! Through equestrian experiences, riders learn a great deal about riding, and about life. Some of what you and I can learn through equestrianism has to do with the technical aspects of riding. No question about it! To learn all of the technical aspects that will take you to where you want to go, however, you need to consider more than just riding technique. In addition, as an aspiring rider, you need also to consider equestrianism from a broader perspective. Riding is one aspect of every equestrian's life. For some of us, riding is a key part of life. For others, riding is peripheral and recreational. For all of us, riding is one of several life aspects. Life is comprised of a wide number of smaller parts, all of which contribute to riding perspective. Riding is not meant to be all consuming for any rider regardless of level and ambition. Riding is meant to be fun for both horse and rider. Riding is part of a style of life that includes exposure to nature, and the ability to communicate, as unlikely as it is, with another species. Riding at its best offers a great many life lessons to each one of us providing we are ready to accept its gifts. Horses are also very communicative. They are meant to remind us of friendship, honesty, sharing of time, the ability to see beyond ourselves, and patience. Take the necessary time each day to notice your horse, yourself, and those around you. The best of equestrian pursuits happen within a bigger picture.

General Tips

- You can optimize your riding performances by adopting a big picture approach to riding. Each ride ought to be considered within a grander scheme of riding progression and life quality.
- Riding provides each one of us with an opportunity to learn about ourselves. Initial riding responses can provide you with insight about the best parts of your riding approach, as well as a few aspects in need of refinement.

- Your horse can provide you with insight regarding your approach to each ride from start to finish providing you pay close attention.
- A balanced approach to riding includes training times, relaxation times, and playing times. All three aspects, in balance, can maintain and restore horse and rider perspective.

9. Closing on equestrian performance

As you can see by now the thinking and feeling aspects of equestrian performance can have a far reaching impact on you, the equestrian. There are many benefits that come from our experiences as equestrians. Some of those benefits are immediately evident. For instance, every rider, sooner or later, struggles with equestrian confidence and benefits from increased belief after meeting a challenging objective on horseback. Equestrianism also offers lessons in planning and organisation. Without all aspects of planning, our progression as aspiring equestrians is jeopardized. The daily plan sets the organisation for each session, the weekly plan ensures a balance of training and lower key relaxation activities, the monthly plan ensures forward movement in terms of individual skills, and yearly and general long-term plans provide clarity and a pathway from present status to future dreams. These few aspects are the anticipated benefits offered by the thinking aspect of equestrian pursuits.

 A good performance is the result of enjoyment, dedication and teamwork: winning is an added bonus.

But wait a minute! Equestrianism offers learning opportunities well beyond what we might have initially anticipated. It offers a vehicle through which we can evaluate our successes, and consider how we bounce back from setbacks. It teaches resilience, more so than many other sports, because equestrianism is humbling. Horses are not meant to bend to the will of human kind in the act of subservience. They are unique entities with their own distinct equestrian needs. Their needs sometimes take each one of us on unanticipated journeys, some uplifting, some frustrating. Equestrianism also teaches each one of us how to set goals, and afterward, how to convince our mounts that our hopes and dreams ought also to be theirs. As you well know, the task of selling a vision is challenging enough for athletes and coaches outside of equestrianism. A group of professional ice hockey and basketball coaches I interviewed early on in my academic career claimed that selling the value of goals to others is the most important and intricate motivational aspect of athletic performance. Imagine trying to sell those goals to an entirely different species with different needs and a different language! Beyond the challenge of goal-setting comes the life lessons gained from forced balance, for instance. The world, we can all agree, is moving quicker with each day. Our world is shrinking, and friends and clients can be communicated with at all corners of the world, daily! The rapid pace that we are faced with holds no relevance to our equestrian partner, the horse. Horses move at their own natural pace, they are clear in the communication of needs, what inspires them, and what troubles them. From the horse, and its ability to return us to nature, we inadvertently learn perspective. There is no escaping the here and now in our favoured sport.

Equestrianism is an amazing sport with too many life lessons to encapsulate in only one book. Its implications are only amazing however provided we stop and pour over its teachings. Every rider, at least initially, approaches riding with the intuitive understanding of its special offerings. For those of us who maintain or retrace its benefits, equestrianism is rewarding beyond its appearance at face value. It is an opportunity for camaraderie, an opportunity for self-reflection, an opportunity to transcend one's own needs, and central to this book, it is an opportunity to package oneself and perform. When I speak of performance, I use the term loosely. Performance is not merely about winning, impressing others, or riding to glory in an Olympic Games, though each of these pursuits has an enjoyable and noble aspect to it.

Performance, in relation to this book, refers to a grander vision. Performance is all about the exceeding of personal limitations and the experiencing of uncharted equestrian territory. Performance is more about the enjoyment you gain from learning new skills, experiencing new setbacks and then rebounding, and it is about the melding of three entities: rider, coach, and horse, into one. The performance lessons that equestrianism offers, in my view, are lessons that will benefit your existence as a whole. This book was meant to spur you onward in the pursuit of equestrian excellence with thinking techniques that are cutting edge, supported by science, and grounded very much in reality.

Moving forward

I am not going to repeat the discussions that were covered in previous chapters. Doing so would probably make for a boring and repetitive close to an interesting series of discussions. As the curtain call to this book, instead, I want to suggest, in brief, some future possibilities for your progression as an inspired and aspiring equestrian. The suggestions we are going to discuss now will be possible solutions to a few additional setbacks encountered within our sport. The setbacks I am speaking of include the following:

* What to do when you reach a standstill in your development;
* How to change a poor habit; and
* How to motivate yourself on the day to day when inspiration wanes.

Each of these final aspects could be chapters in and of themselves, but that is not the intention here. Instead, consider this final parting discussion as a troubleshooting handbook with suggestions for rerouted performance.

Reaching a standstill

During my last book, Focused Riding, there was mention of the term "plateau". All equestrians, at one time or another, feel that they have reached a standstill. It appears to each of us during those trying moments that no matter how much effort we exert no forward movement results. Increases in effort and emotional investment take us nowhere. Riders look to coaches for reassurance, as parents, mates and friends share in their frustration. During those typical moments, some equestrians, not unlike enthusiasts from other sport, question whether they have the ability to succeed. Self-questioning and uncertainty is often followed up with declines in effort, and sometimes riders step away from their sport, at least for the short-term.

Slumps might result from technical errors, but they are continued through negative thoughts, negative feelings, and negative actions.

The answer to performance standstills is not always easy to uncover. However, such moments provide the well informed equestrian with an opportunity to press their thinking and feelings skills into action. In every sport through to the professional level, athletes and coaches experience performance slumps. The term slump indicates that there is little that can be done when performance halts other than accept its onslaught. Perhaps so! However, acceptance of the performance standstill only takes the performer part way to the end solution of resumed progress. Acceptance is beneficial, because often, when we struggle, energy is misspent on frustration and the continued re-imaging of technical and tactically poor decisions. Slumps might result from technical errors, but they are continued through negative thoughts, negative feelings, and negative actions. Should you ever experience a performance standstill, I suggest you consider it in relation to all of the previous chapters. For instance, are you perpetuating your poor performance with negative thoughts and problem oriented thinking? You can also consider whether your slump has been caused by a missing step within your goal-setting process. Or how about this: are you reinforcing your standstill by re-imaging poor performance and adding to your current level of frustration? What of the plan you have been using for performance? Has it been optimal, and has it been founded on a broad enough base of preparatory skills? Finally, where are you currently in terms of performance perspective? Are you still using your balanced approach to training and performance? The questions and answers posed by every one of the previous chapters will at least take you part of

the way to restored performance. Don't forget what you have learned! After all, in the introduction I mentioned that thinking skills are waxed skills. They need to be used, and they need to be used regularly in order for them to work in full measure.

Changing a habit

Another frustration experienced by many an equestrian is the struggle to change weak habits. Sometimes we develop weak riding habits such as a poor posture, a mistimed aid, and even a weak mental habit, such as second guessing. If you have ever tried changing a weak habit, you certainly know how hard that task can be. I struggled for years with my left wrist, which always seemed to take on a life of its own, turning counter clockwise until it was completely horizontal instead of vertical. No matter what I did, it seemed that the irritating tendency persisted for almost two decades. In hindsight and through study, I have come to realize that habits can persist for a very long time, and the longer they persist, the more challenging they are to right. I have been witness to many a coach frustrated by riders with a persisting habit. Coaches often misinterpret the rider's recurring habit as the result of too little effort, and a lack of focus. And so, in response, the coach's effort sometimes wanes. Habits, good and bad, are common to all sports including equestrianism, and often, the question becomes how to change those that undermine performance.

Weak habits tend to have lifecycles of their own, as a leading motivational psychologist James Prochaska has indicated over the last decade. They originate unintentionally, but their replacement with better ones must be deliberate. At first, we are unaware of the less than optimal equestrian habit. Next, we learn of our weakness as a result of personal experience, or often, through coaching sug-

Changing a performance hindering bad habit, such as looking down over a jump, takes time but can be done.

gestion. Afterward, we decide to change the weak behaviour, gather all of the necessary knowledge and tools to do so, and attack. From then on, habits are altered and monitored until new and improved habits formalize. Though change sounds relatively simple, for many of us its process can take a long time to happen. First of all, riders and coaches have to recognize that the behaviour is undermining of equestrian performance. Then, the importance of changing the habit must become a priority. Once a weak habit becomes a priority, its change typically requires at least six months of technical supervision, and more truthfully, upwards of two years. Finally, the transition of a weaker habit to one that is performance enhancing requires upwards of five years of occasional monitoring by rider and coach. Given the challenges faced by any equestrian desiring changes in technique or tactic, the chances of refinement are sometimes less than we anticipate.

Refinements are important to every equestrian's development. Weak habits are simply behaviours in need of refinement. Slight changes in technique and tactic, when you need to make them, will require consistent mindfulness and monitoring. To remain mindful during each day's ride, you can use my favourite tool: index cards. Write your habit reminder in the positive, with a suggestion of what to do. Be solution focused! In addition, ensure that all coaching feedback is solution focused, as well. When riders are told what to do, constructive messages create hope and an image of what needs to be done. In addition, start integrating key statements as reminders. One example of a key statement for the rider who slouches is 'sit straight' or 'carry yourself'. Both are positive reminders of what needs to be focused on in the present moment. In addition, mirrors and video footage provide useful information of how your newly developed change is taking root. On the day to day, if they are available, refer to mirrors. Mirrors are honest, and they are accurate providing you are prepared to listen to their message. Over the long-term, purchase a videotape, and have your coach or a friend tape you on occasion, preferably without your knowing. If you are modifying and refining a habit, it should show a progression over time. Finally, return to the content we have discussed in previous chapters as foundation tools. Remember to be optimistic and persistent, remember to be confident that change can happen, remember to monitor your improvements over time, remember to reinforce good riding through good imagery, and remember to test your refined habit in ever changing circumstances. Again, press your knowledge into action. You are capable of phenomenal improvements providing you use what you know!

Day to day motivation

As you will agree, equestrianism is a phenomenal sport. It is not hard to become inspired within our sport, in part because horses are generous with their time and their abilities. Despite the love of equestrianism that all horse people share, each one of us will experience some amount of motivational decline sooner or later. Have you ever experienced the ebb and flow in your motivation as an equestrian? If you are anything like me, you have probably experienced more energy and ambition on some days of riding than on others. There are simply days when each one of us is more excited about riding in comparison to others. Feelings of boredom can happen to the best among us despite a perfect balance of formal schooling with out of doors riding, and fun and games. There are also times when each of us is left to ride alone in poor weather, times when we are overtired, times when we are overwhelmed with life's demands, and times when today's task feels just like yesterday's. Sometimes we misplace the excitement that equestrian performance deserves, and it frustrates us.

When experiencing declines in energy, or a momentary loss of passion, many of the clients I have coached and consulted with have mentioned feelings of guilt and shame. After all, our horses wait for us each day with the positive expectation of another ride, and more shared time. Contributing to our personal turmoil are the added thoughts of previous emotional and financial investment. Coupled together, motivational declines and responding perceptions that end with obligatory rides chip away at our earliest of equestrian feelings: passion. Passion is, perhaps, the most important emotional aspect of stellar sport performance, and when it is misplaced, so too is the essential ingredient of emotional investment. Equestrians need to feel emotionally invested and passionate toward their sport and all of its aspects in order to remain fully committed. Too often, riders forget about their initial passion never to rediscover the motivational aspects of the horse world.

Luckily, as you retrace each chapter, there are many ways to inspire motivation even in moments

Motivational decline can be the result of sub-par performance, over-tiredness or loss of enthusiasm. All those are temporary phenomena.

that are ordinary. Reminders of your progression over time will trigger thoughts of progression, and the pride that goes along with it. Optimism also has a lot to offer in times of motivational lapse. A pessimistic equestrian might respond to losses of excitement with the response that they are losing interest. The optimist, on the other hand would argue to the contrary. Taking a page from the optimist's handbook, you can simply consider short-term declines as exactly that: short-term and thus short lived. Just because you are not excited about equestrianism today does not mean that you will

not be excited about equestrianism tomorrow! Moving onward through the book's content, inspiring images and video footage of your best rides and the rides of other people succeeding in what you want to do can serve as inspirational. From the arousal chapter, all you might need for inspiration is a little excitement. Perhaps you are under-aroused today, and in desperate need of an exciting and challenging activity to serve as stimulation. How often have you anticipated a boring activity in your day only to find yourself enjoying it because someone or something has brought momentary energy to the setting? Finally, a balanced approach to equestrianism would suggest that there will be mundane days in every aspect of your life from time to time, including equestrianism. To assume otherwise would be unrealistic. During those instances, I suppose, your challenge is to discover or re-discover something unique and inspirational during the mundane moment. One thought I always reflected on when I had to push through a day's training as a teenager, was that 'this is my opportunity to gain an edge on the competition'. I wagered with myself that no one else trained consistently when they didn't want to or need to. Exceptional performance in any sport including equestrianism, to be honest with you, happens as a result of an internal ambition despite the acknowledgement that we will be more inspired on some days than on others. The final word, I suppose, is to persist on the day to day, and afterward, to dwell on the positives that persistent behaviour offers.

◎ Declines in enthusiasm or loss of passion are often accompanied by feelings of guilt driven by our expectations and those of our horses and back-up teams.

Parting words

I suppose in closing, it is worth asking what we both have learned from our shared time together as inspired equestrians. I hope that you, as I did, have realized that the thinking part of equestrianism is all about discovery and re-discovery. My guess is that you have probably learned a few new tricks as a result of this book; at least I hope you did! There were a lot of different exercises and scenarios discussed over the ten chapters of this book's content. In relation to the new tools that you have learned, don't become overwhelmed by the vast quantity of possibilities. There are undoubtedly too many tools for you to press all of them into play right now. My guess is that you have already placed more priority on a few of our discussed topics at this moment. That is fine. Now that you have a familiarity with several topics, prioritize those that are most important right now. The other topics will not go away, or fade from print. You can return to them down the road as they become more important. Rest assured, sooner or later, you will find substance in every topic, and sooner or later you will be tempted to try exercises that you might not opt to try right now.

There will also be discussions that you have probably heard before, elsewhere. Perhaps the skills I touched on were skills that someone taught you earlier on, skills that you have forgotten about. Isn't it great to rediscover meaningful lessons that have been lost to time and memory? Learning tends to work that way, especially in the area of thinking and motivational strategies. The rediscovering of old lessons is much like the rediscovery of an old and familiar hat. As hindsight, once we have retraced old memories, we often wonder why we let them go in the first place, they seem so comfortable. For the instances that you have re-learned something from the days of old, good for you! Now that you have returned to techniques that worked for you earlier, use them deliberately, and promise yourself that you will not misplace them again. Remember that what worked for you before will often work for you again. As the saying goes 'don't fix what isn't broken'.

Finally, it is my hope that, if nothing else, this book has re-affirmed that you do know how to think and perform optimally based on earlier experiences. It is only a matter of repeating what works time and again for performance to follow. Again, with an increased awareness of what works, do more of it time and again. It is important that you develop a solid and complete mental game plan when the goal is equestrian performance. It makes no difference whether you are an inspired recreational equestrian or an aspiring competitive equestrian. Integrate the skills that you know work, and do them as often as you can. As we discussed earlier, good experiences build on good experiences. Success is founded on earlier success much like a house is built from the best of foundations, upward. At times, at least initially, you might find it challenging to integrate all of the correct techniques that you know will work. Integrate as many of them as you can, and slowly, add to your base of correct skills. Before long, your equestrian performance will be more complete than even you imagined.

Now, we have come full circle in our discussion of equestrian performance. You certainly began your riding pursuits with optimism, clear goals, positive images, a plan, some perspective, and a beginner's mindset. As a parting memory, this book is meant to return you to the very same intuitive thoughts that you began with. Though there is no one answer to great equestrian experiences, with a pinch of optimism, a few confidence skills, a clear vision, a few arousal skills, a couple of performance tricks, a healthy perspective, and most important, a beginner's mindset, you will do great! Rest assured that you already knew much of what we have spoken about here. But then again, there is a difference between knowing of and knowing through lived experience. It is now time for you to press your skills into action. If you haven't already done so, put this book down for now, and have a great ride!

Acknowledgements

It is currently the end of my third year as a cross appointed psychology and sport psychology professor at Laurentian University. On reflection, I must full heartedly acknowledge Laurentian's support of my academic and applied sport psychology endeavours. I would also like to thank one central person who started me down the path of high-performance sport consulting, Dr Matt Mizerski, my good friend and mentor. Your sage wisdom has been nothing short of profound. Gratitude is also extended to my family for introducing me to the wonderful world of horses, and more specifically, the talented mounts I had the privilege to compete with. I am also grateful for the friendship of my mother-in-law, Kelly, someone I enjoy visiting with regularly. Finally, I would like to thank the many athletes and coaches who shared their experiences and insights with me. I promise that you have taught me well, and that I will continue to learn from your teachings.

The publishers would also like to thank the following for their assistance with the photographs for this book:

Alec and Emily Lohore, the staff and horses at Burnham Market Eventing Centre.

Meryl Doran, the liveries and their horses at The Old Stables, Godden Green, Kent.

The Ely Eventing Centre and the competitors at the Little Downham One-Day Event.

Robert Schinke, in march 2006

About the author

Robert Schinke first started as an equestrian at the age of nine. Since, he has competed at international level, first as a four-time American Continental Young Rider, and afterward, at senior level as a member of the Canadian Equestrian Team. Later, on scholarship, Rob completed a Masters with a specialization in Sport Psychology, and a Doctorate in Education, for which he researched the effects of support-system optimism on national team athlete performance during major international competitions. Rob has produced more than 150 academic and applied publications and presentations to this point in his career. He has worked with national teams and professional sport affiliates in Canada and abroad for more than ten years. As an academic, Rob is an internationally recognized sport psychology professor and researcher teaching at Laurentian University, in Sudbury, Canada. He is a member of the Canadian Mental Training Registry, a Social Science and Humanities Research Council grant recipient, the Co-Editor for Athletic Insight, the online journal of sport psychology, and the Book Review Editor for Avante, the academic journal for the Canadian Association of Physical Education, Recreation and Dance. Rob lives in Sudbury, Ontario, Canada with his wife Erin, and his dogs Blitzen and Seal.